Nathan Goodman

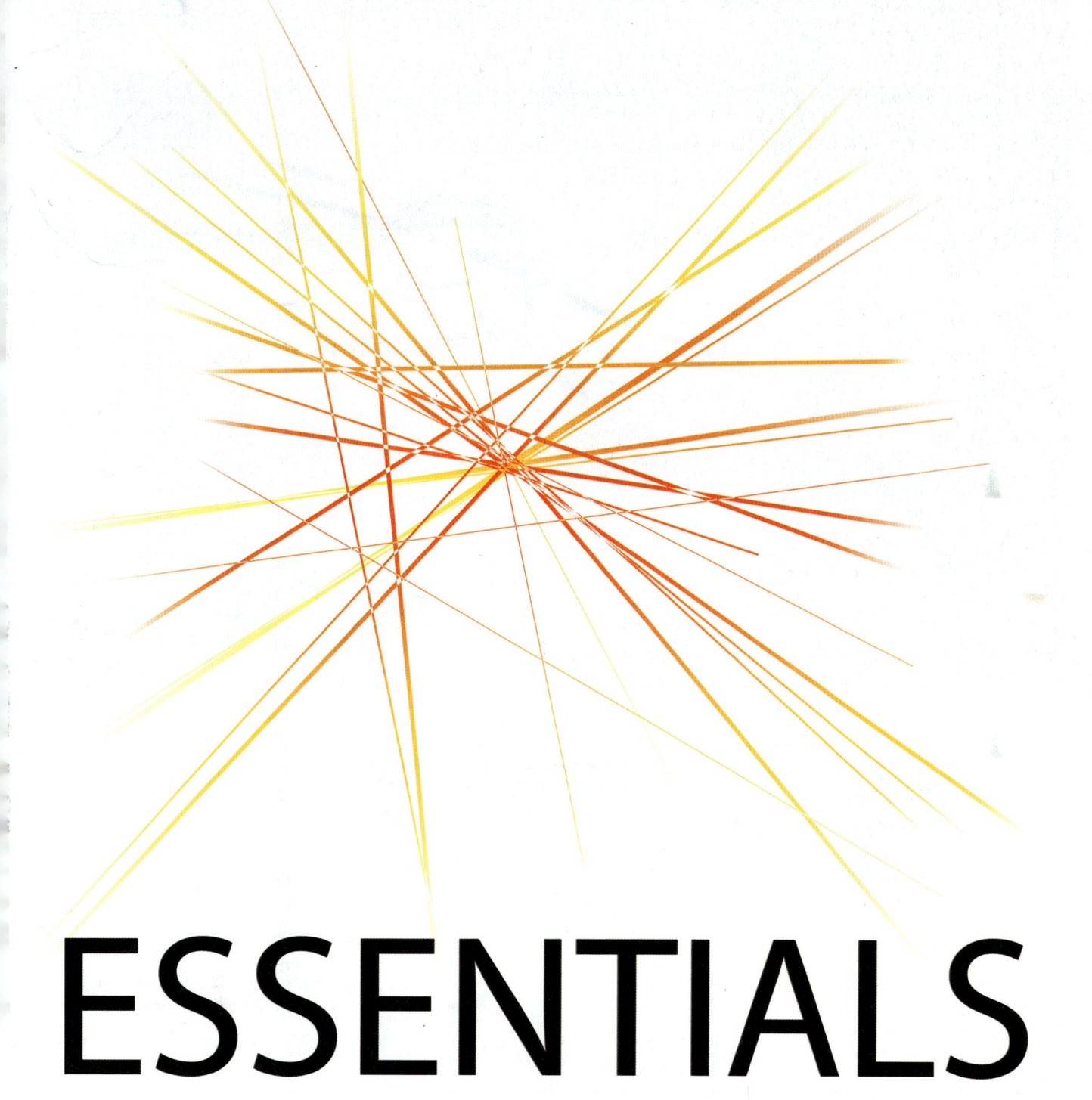

ESSENTIALS

OCR Twenty First Century
GCSE Physics
Revision Guide

Contents

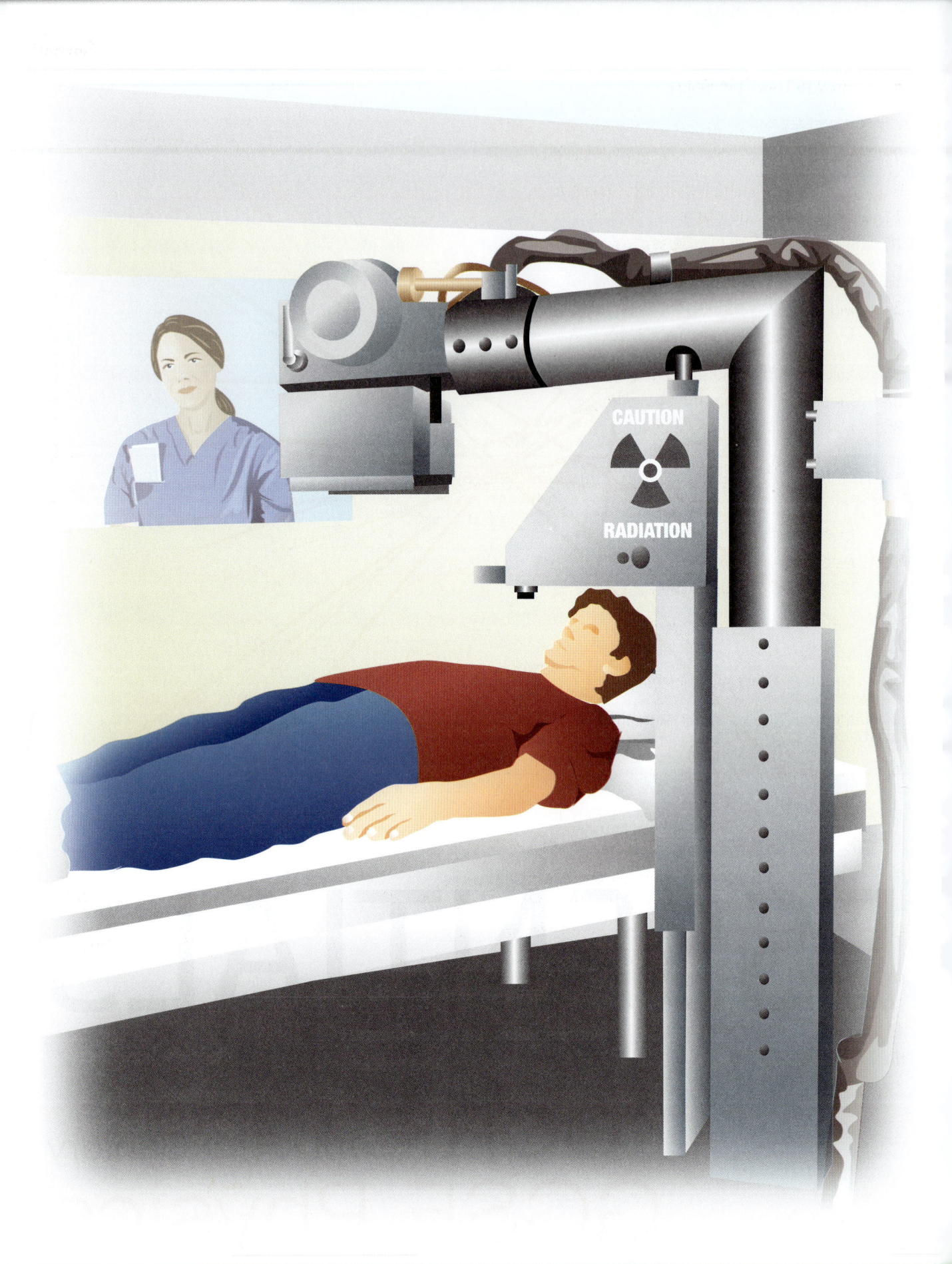

Contents

Revised

4 How to Use This Guide

Unit 1

- **6** Module P1: The Earth in the Universe
- **14** Module P1 Summary
- **16** Module P1 Practice Questions
- **18** Module P2: Radiation and Life
- **24** Module P2 Summary
- **26** Module P2 Practice Questions
- **28** Module P3: Radioactive Materials
- **36** Module P3 Summary
- **38** Module P3 Practice Questions

Unit 2

- **40** Module P4: Explaining Motion
- **48** Module P4 Summary
- **50** Module P4 Practice Questions
- **52** Module P5: Electric Circuits
- **60** Module P5 Summary
- **62** Module P5 Practice Questions
- **64** Module P6: The Wave Model of Radiation
- **72** Module P6 Summary
- **74** Module P6 Practice Questions

Unit 3

- **76** Module P7: Further Physics, Observing the Universe
- **92** Module P7 Summary
- **94** Module P7 Practice Questions

- **96** Glossary of Key Words
- **99** Answers to Practice Questions
- **104** Index
- **IBC** Acknowledgements

How to Use This Guide

How to Use This Guide

This revision guide has been written and developed to help you get the most out of your revision. This guide covers both Foundation and Higher Tier content.

HT Content that will only be tested on the Higher Tier papers appears in a pale yellow tinted box labelled with the **HT** symbol.

- The **coloured page headers** clearly identify the separate units, so that you can revise for each one separately.
- There are **practice questions** at the end of each module so you can test yourself on what you've just learned. (The answers are given on pages 99–101 so you can mark your own answers.)
- You'll find **key words** in a yellow box on each two-page spread. They are also highlighted in colour within the text; Higher Tier key words are highlighted in orange. Make sure you know and understand all these words before moving on!
- There's a **glossary** at the back of the book. It contains the key words from throughout the book so you can check any definitions you're unsure of.
- The **tick boxes** on the contents pages let you track your revision progress: simply put a tick in the box next to each topic when you're confident that you know it.
- Don't just read the guide – **learn actively**! Constantly test yourself without looking at the text.

Good luck with your exams!

Nathan Goodman has an in-depth understanding of the new science specifications, thanks to his roles as Secondary Science Strategy Consultant for North East Lincolnshire LEA and Regional Coordinator at the Institute of Physics for the physics teacher network. As Assistant Headteacher, Nathan is involved in improving the teaching and learning of science at his current school.

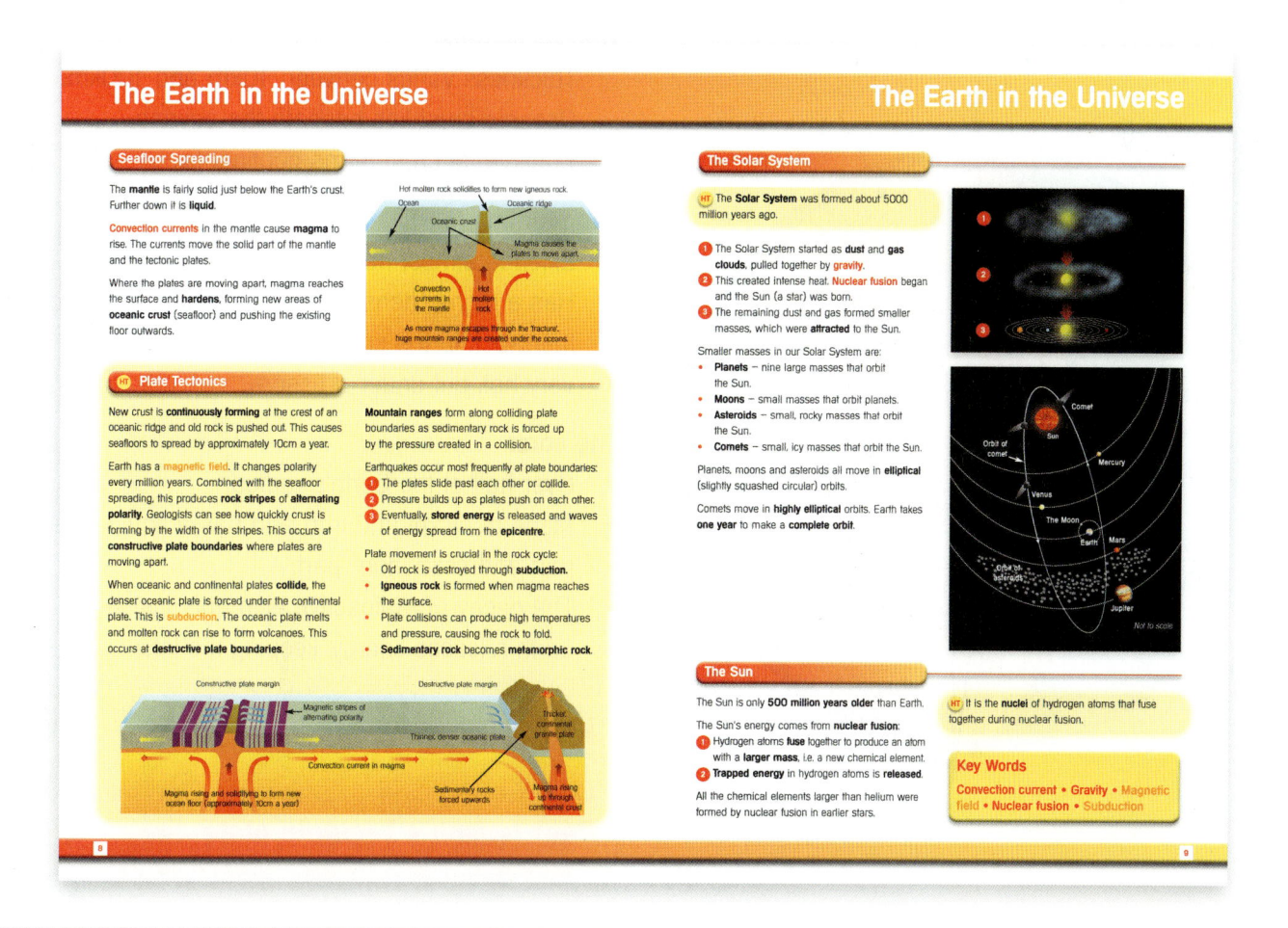

The Earth in the Universe

The Earth

When it first formed, Earth was completely **molten** (hot liquid). Scientists estimate Earth is **4500 million** years old as it has to be older than its oldest rocks.

HT The oldest rocks found on Earth are about 4000 million years old.

Studying rocks tells us more about the Earth's structure and how it has changed as a result of the following processes:

- **Erosion** – the Earth's surface is made of **rock layers,** one on top of another. The oldest is at the bottom. The layers are **compacted sediment**, produced by weathering and erosion. Erosion changes the surface over time.
- **Craters** – the Moon's surface is covered with **impact craters** from meteors. Meteors also hit the Earth but craters have been erased by erosion.
- **Mountain formation** – if new mountains weren't being formed the Earth's surface would have eroded down to sea level.
- **Folding** – some rocks look as if they have been folded in half. This required huge force over a long time.

Further evidence of the Earth's age can be found by studying…

- **fossils** of plants and animals in **sedimentary rock layers**, which show how life's changed
- the **radioactivity** of rocks. A rock's **radioactivity** decreases over time and radioactive dating measures radiation levels to find out a rock's age.

The Structure of the Earth

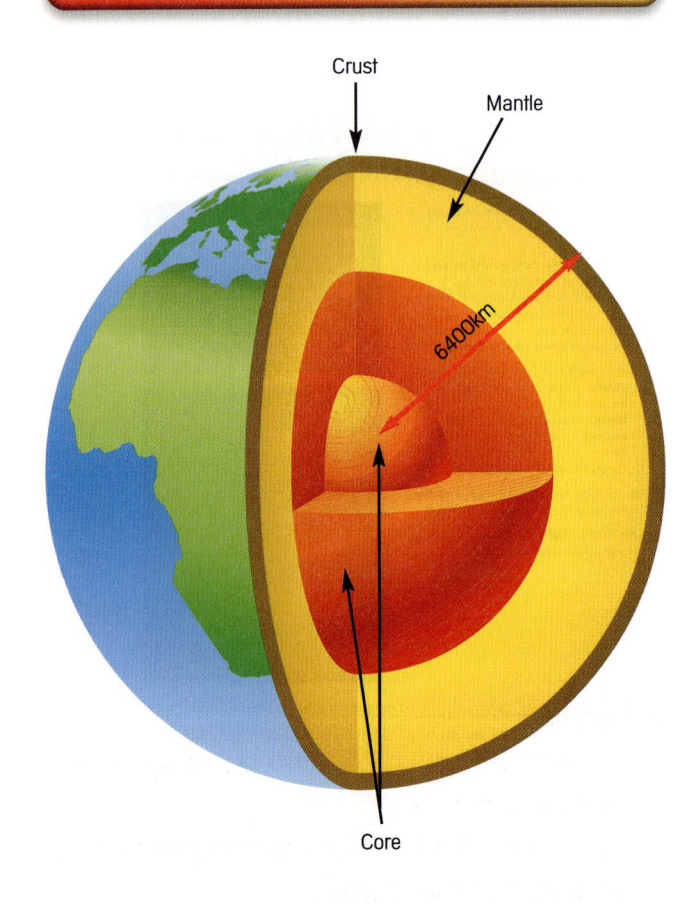

Thin rocky crust:
- Thickness varies between 10km and 100km.
- Oceanic crust lies beneath the oceans.
- Continental crust forms continents.

The mantle:
- Extends almost halfway to the centre.
- Has a higher density, and different composition, than rock in the crust.
- Very hot, but under pressure.

The core:
- Over half of the Earth's radius.
- Made of nickel and iron and has a liquid outer part and solid inner part.
- The decay of radioactive elements inside the Earth releases energy, keeping the interior hot.

Key Words

Continental drift • Erosion • Geohazard • Peer review • Tectonic plate

The Earth in the Universe

Continental Drift

Continental drift theory was proposed by **Wegener**. He saw that the continents had a jigsaw fit, with mountain ranges and rock patterns **matching up**.

There were also fossils of the same animals on different continents. He said that different continents had separated and drifted apart. Wegener also claimed that when two continents collided they forced each other upwards to make mountains.

Geologists didn't accept Wegener's theory because…
- he wasn't a geologist so was seen as an outsider
- the supporting evidence was limited
- it could be explained more simply, e.g. a bridge connecting continents had eroded over time
- the movement of the continents wasn't detectable.

Evidence from seafloor spreading finally convinced the scientific community that Wegener was correct. Through this **peer review** process it became an accepted theory.

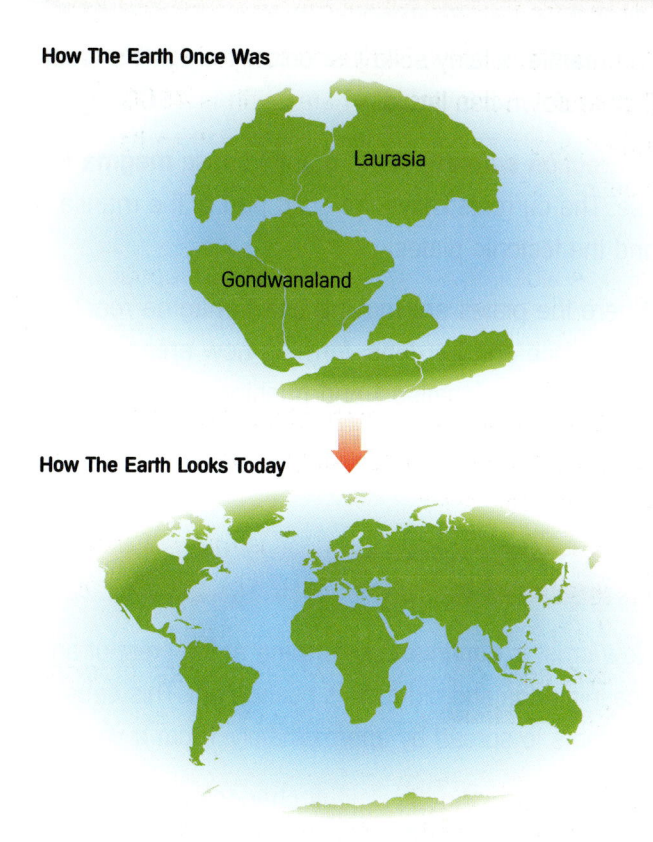

How The Earth Once Was

Laurasia

Gondwanaland

How The Earth Looks Today

Tectonic Plates

The Earth's crust is cracked into several large pieces called **tectonic plates**. The plates…
- float on the Earth's **mantle** as they're less dense
- can move apart, move towards, or slide past each other.

The lines where plates meet are called **plate boundaries**. **Volcanoes**, **earthquakes** and **mountain formations** normally occur at these plate boundaries.

Earthquakes near coastlines or at sea can often result in a **tsunami** (a tidal wave).

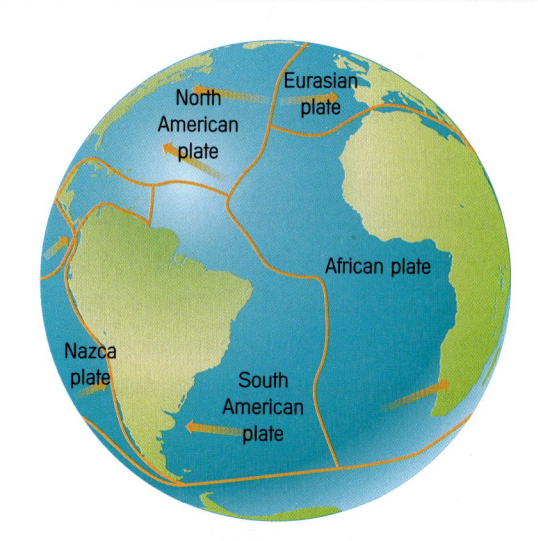

North American plate
Eurasian plate
African plate
Nazca plate
South American plate

Geohazards

A **geohazard** is a **natural hazard**, e.g. floods and hurricanes. Some have warning signs which give authorities time to evacuate the area, use sandbags, etc.

However, others strike without warning so **precautionary measures** need to be taken.

For example…
- buildings in earthquake zones are designed to withstand tremors
- authorities will often refuse planning permission in areas prone to flooding.

The Earth in the Universe

Seafloor Spreading

The **mantle** is fairly solid just below the Earth's crust. Further down it is **liquid**.

Convection currents in the mantle cause **magma** to rise. The currents move the solid part of the mantle and the tectonic plates.

Where the plates are moving apart, magma reaches the surface and **hardens**, forming new areas of **oceanic crust** (seafloor) and pushing the existing floor outwards.

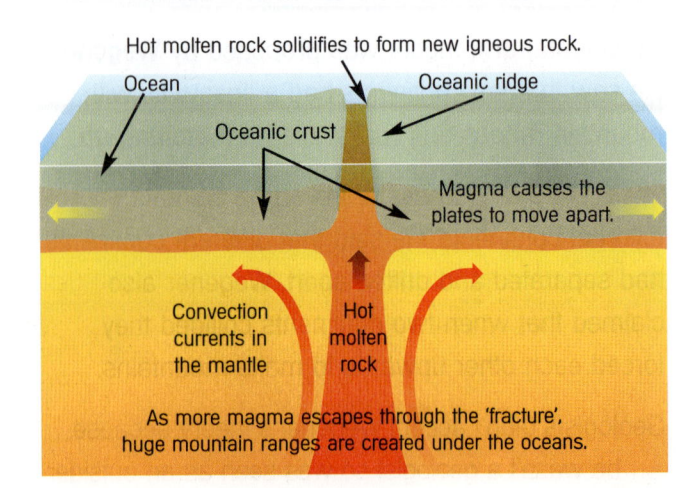

HT Plate Tectonics

New crust is **continuously forming** at the crest of an oceanic ridge and old rock is pushed out. This causes seafloors to spread by approximately 10cm a year.

Earth has a **magnetic field**. It changes polarity every million years. Combined with the seafloor spreading, this produces **rock stripes** of **alternating polarity**. Geologists can see how quickly crust is forming by the width of the stripes. This occurs at **constructive plate boundaries** where plates are moving apart.

When oceanic and continental plates **collide**, the denser oceanic plate is forced under the continental plate. This is **subduction**. The oceanic plate melts and molten rock can rise to form volcanoes. This occurs at **destructive plate boundaries**.

Mountain ranges form along colliding plate boundaries as sedimentary rock is forced up by the pressure created in a collision.

Earthquakes occur most frequently at plate boundaries:
1. The plates slide past each other or collide.
2. Pressure builds up as plates push on each other.
3. Eventually, **stored energy** is released and waves of energy spread from the **epicentre**.

Plate movement is crucial in the rock cycle:
- Old rock is destroyed through **subduction.**
- **Igneous rock** is formed when magma reaches the surface.
- Plate collisions can produce high temperatures and pressure, causing the rock to fold.
- **Sedimentary rock** becomes **metamorphic rock**.

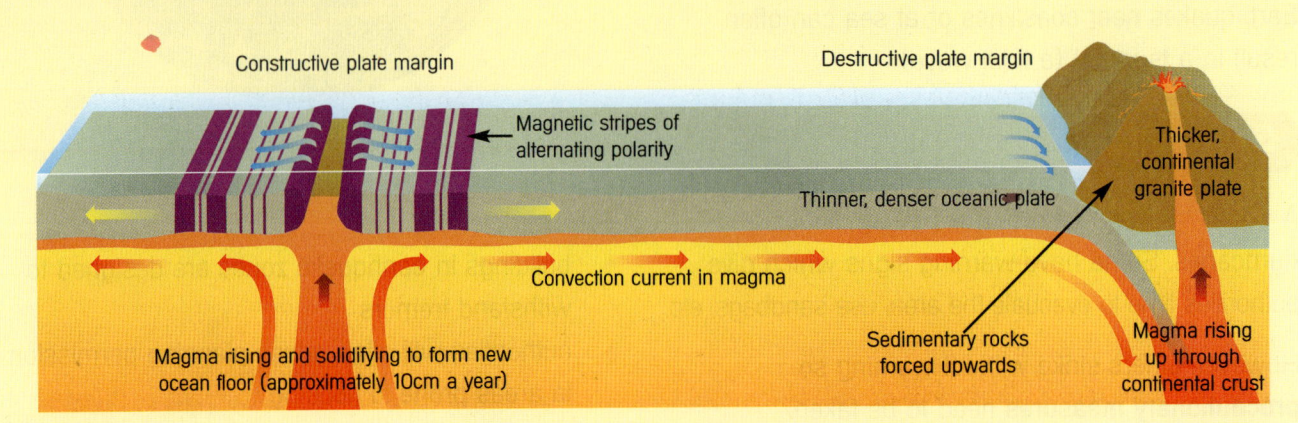

The Earth in the Universe

The Solar System

HT The **Solar System** was formed about 5000 million years ago.

1. The Solar System started as **dust** and **gas clouds**, pulled together by **gravity**.
2. This created intense heat. **Nuclear fusion** began and the Sun (a star) was born.
3. The remaining dust and gas formed smaller masses, which were **attracted** to the Sun.

Smaller masses in our Solar System are:
- **Planets** – nine large masses that orbit the Sun.
- **Moons** – small masses that orbit planets.
- **Asteroids** – small, rocky masses that orbit the Sun.
- **Comets** – small, icy masses that orbit the Sun.

Planets, moons and asteroids all move in **elliptical** (slightly squashed circular) orbits.

Comets move in **highly elliptical** orbits. Earth takes **one year** to make a **complete orbit**.

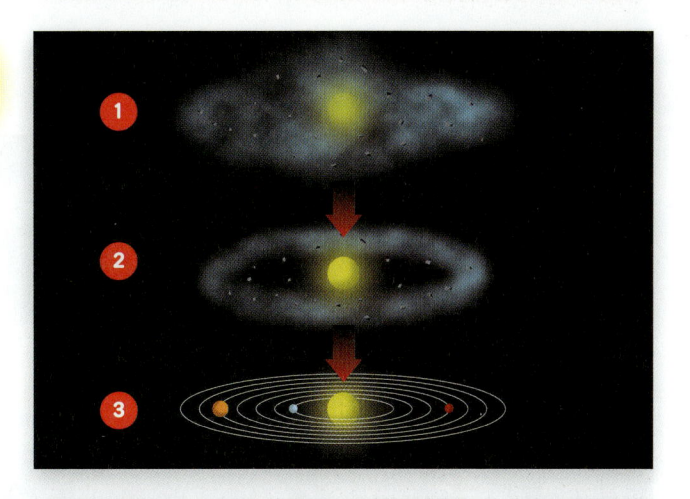

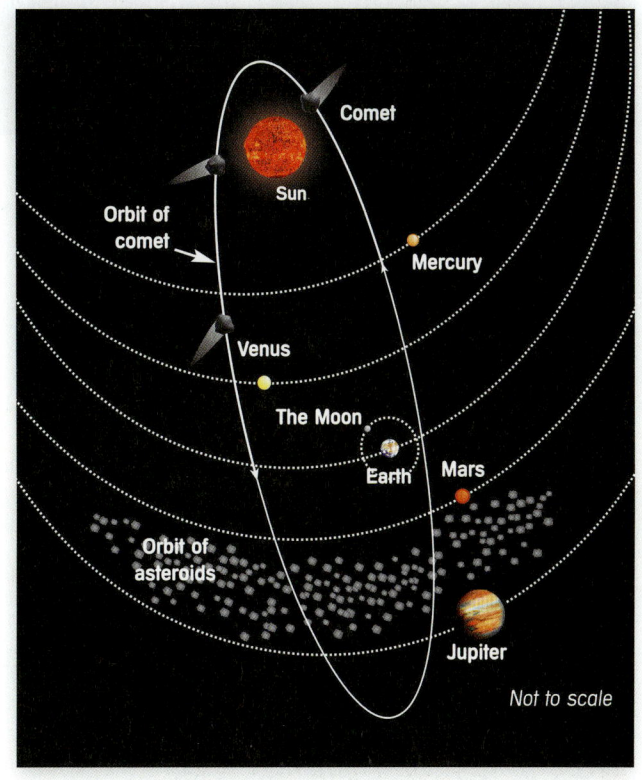

The Sun

The Sun is only **500 million years older** than Earth.

The Sun's energy comes from **nuclear fusion**:
1. Hydrogen atoms **fuse** together to produce an atom with a **larger mass**, i.e. a new chemical element.
2. **Trapped energy** in hydrogen atoms is **released**.

All the chemical elements larger than helium were formed by nuclear fusion in earlier stars.

HT It is the **nuclei** of hydrogen atoms that fuse together during nuclear fusion.

Key Words

Convection current • Gravity • Magnetic field • Nuclear fusion • Subduction

The Earth in the Universe

The Universe

The Universe is much older than the Sun, approximately **14 000 million years** old.

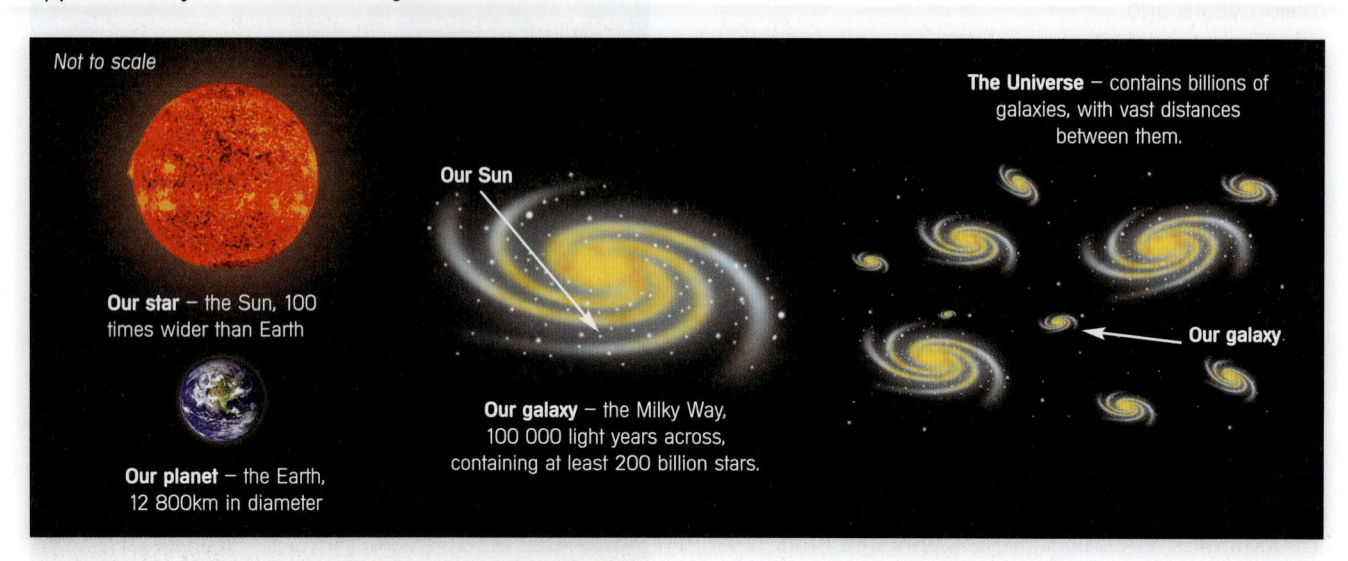

Not to scale

Our star – the Sun, 100 times wider than Earth

Our planet – the Earth, 12 800km in diameter

Our Sun

Our galaxy – the Milky Way, 100 000 light years across, containing at least 200 billion stars.

The Universe – contains billions of galaxies, with vast distances between them.

Our galaxy

The Speed of Light

Light travels at very high but **finite** (limited) speeds. If the distance is great enough, **light speed** can be measured.

HT The **speed of light** is **300 000km/s** (around 1 million times faster than sound). Light from Earth takes just over 1 second to reach the Moon (approximately 384 400km).

Sunlight takes 8 minutes to reach Earth. When we look at the Sun we see it as it was 8 minutes earlier.

Vast space distances are measured in **light years**. One light year is the distance light travels in one year (approximately 9500 billion km).

The nearest galaxy to the **Milky Way** is 2.2 million light years away.

Measuring Distances in Space

Distances are measured in **two** ways:

1. **Relative brightness** – the **dimmer** a star, the **further away** it is. However, brightness can vary so a star's distance is never certain.
2. **Parallax** – if you hold a finger at arm's length and close each eye in turn, your finger appears to move. The closer your finger, the more it seems to move. Parallax uses this idea to work out distance. Stars in the near distance appear to move against the background of distant stars. The closer they are, the more they appear to move. The further the star, the less accurate the measurement is.

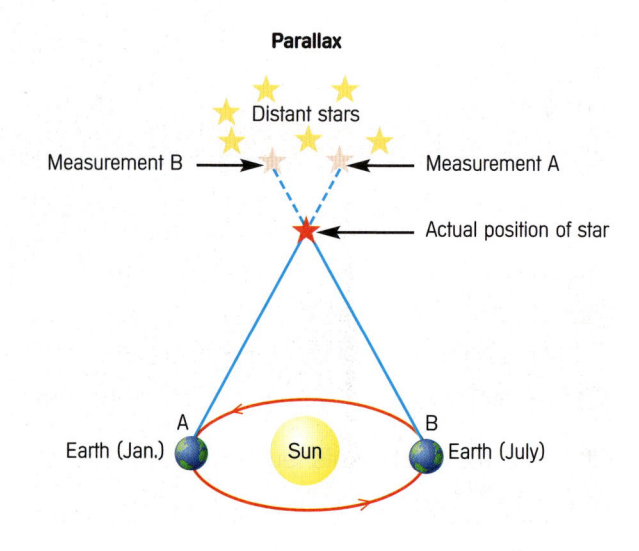

Parallax

Distant stars

Measurement B → ← Measurement A

← Actual position of star

A — B
Earth (Jan.) Sun Earth (July)

The Earth in the Universe

Distant Stars

Radiation from stars tells us what we know about them. Types of radiation that stars produce include **visible light**, **ultraviolet** and **infrared**. **Light pollution** is when electric lights on Earth make it difficult to see the stars. The Hubble Space Telescope orbits at a height of 600km, so it's not affected by this.

The Life Cycle of a Star

All stars consist of hydrogen and have a **finite life**:
1. When a star's hydrogen supply eventually runs out, it **swells** and becomes **colder**.
2. It then forms a **red giant** or a **red super giant**, depending on its size.

Key Words
Light speed • Light year • Neutron star • Radiation • Supernova

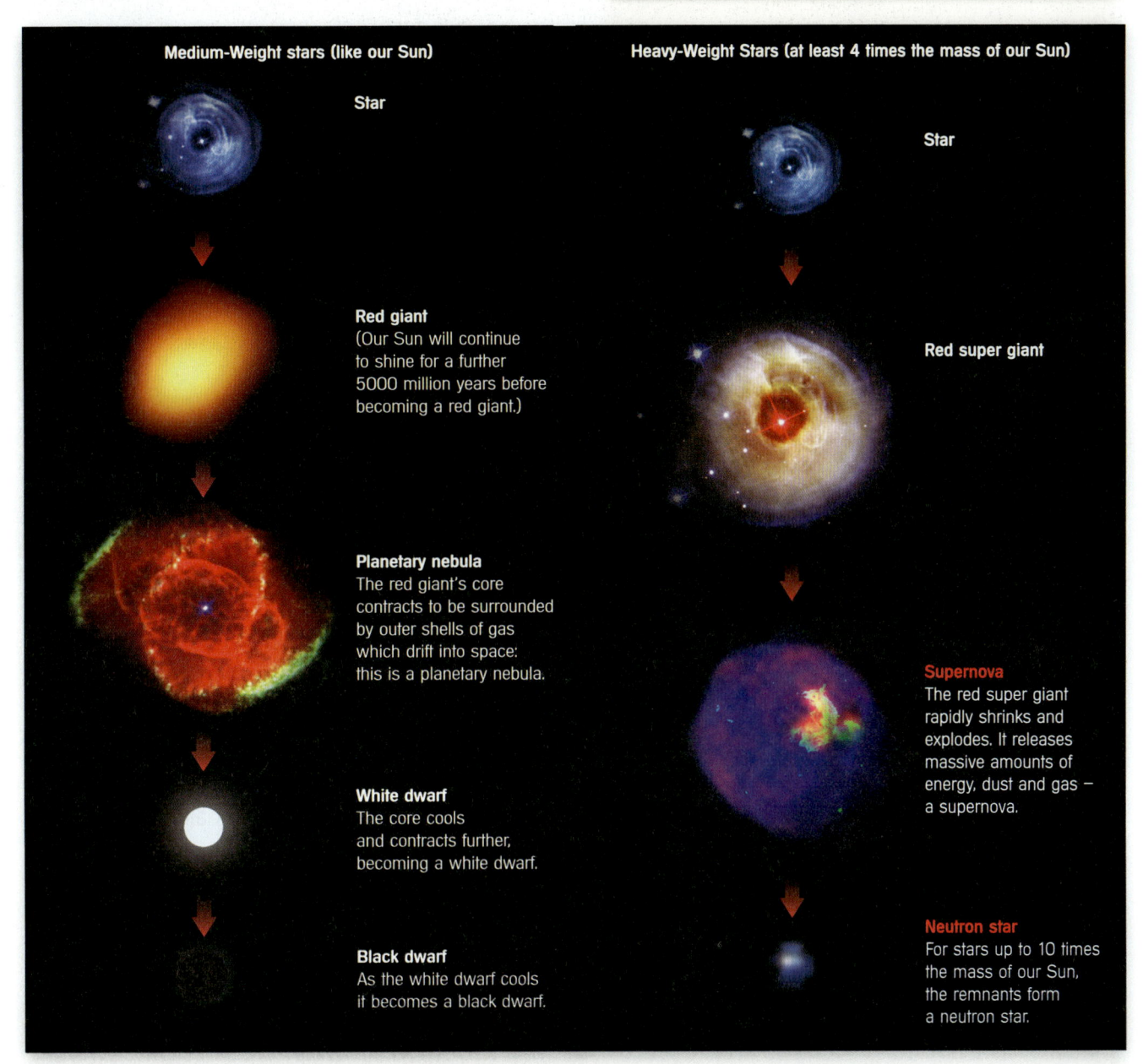

Medium-Weight stars (like our Sun)

Star

↓

Red giant
(Our Sun will continue to shine for a further 5000 million years before becoming a red giant.)

↓

Planetary nebula
The red giant's core contracts to be surrounded by outer shells of gas which drift into space: this is a planetary nebula.

↓

White dwarf
The core cools and contracts further, becoming a white dwarf.

↓

Black dwarf
As the white dwarf cools it becomes a black dwarf.

Heavy-Weight Stars (at least 4 times the mass of our Sun)

Star

↓

Red super giant

↓

Supernova
The red super giant rapidly shrinks and explodes. It releases massive amounts of energy, dust and gas – a supernova.

↓

Neutron star
For stars up to 10 times the mass of our Sun, the remnants form a neutron star.

The Earth in the Universe

Other Galaxies

If a source of light is **moving away** from us, the wavelengths of light are **longer** than if the source is stationary.

Wavelengths of light from nearby galaxies are longer than scientists expect. This means the galaxies are **moving away** from us.

HT Observations made by **Edwin Hubble** showed that almost all galaxies are moving away from us and the further away they are, the faster they are moving away. He developed this into **Hubble's Law** which states:

The speed at which a galaxy is moving away is proportional to its distance.

If all the galaxies are moving away from us, this must mean that space is **expanding**.

The Beginning and The End

The **Big Bang** theory says that the Universe began with a huge explosion 14 000 million years ago.

The future of the Universe depends on its amount of mass. Measuring the amount of mass is difficult so its fate is hard to predict. If there **isn't enough** mass the Universe will keep **expanding**.

If there's **too much** mass, gravity will pull everything back together and the Universe will **collapse**.

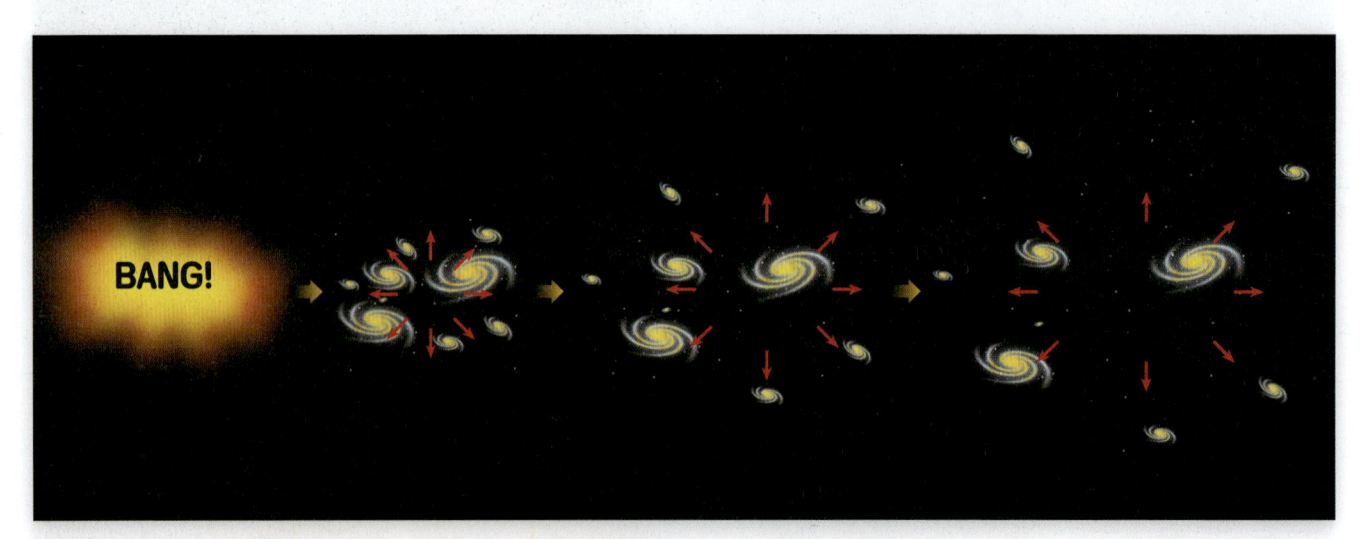

Aliens

In 1996, a Mars meteorite appeared to contain an **ancient alien fossil**. Different explanations were offered but the debate still rages on.

If there are other life forms in the Universe they are likely to be on other planets or moons. Astronomers have detected some stars with orbiting planets.

There's no confirmed evidence of alien life. Many scientists think that with the vast numbers of stars and galaxies, it's unlikely that only Earth has life.

Key Words
Big Bang • Hubble's Law

The Earth in the Universe

What Killed the Dinosaurs?

Evidence shows that dinosaurs became extinct around 65 million years ago. One explanation is that an **asteroid** hit Earth.

The Facts:
- Fossils show that dinosaurs gradually died out.
- The chances of a large asteroid hitting Earth are very small.
- If an asteroid did hit Earth, everything in the **impact zone** would be destroyed.
- Large asteroids have hit Earth in the past. The Chicxulub crater in Mexico provides evidence of this. Scientists estimate the energy of this asteroid on impact was **10 000 times greater** than all the world's nuclear weapons combined.
- A layer of **iridium** (a metallic element common in asteroids) is found all over Earth.

The Explanations:
- The layer of iridium could be the result of an **asteroid collision**.
- A big asteroid would have caused **firestorms**, **shock waves** and possibly climate change. Dinosaurs couldn't have survived.
- The collision could have **released sulfur** and caused **strong acid rain** for weeks.
- Dust could have blocked the Sun and caused plants to die, affecting the whole food chain.

Scientific Explanation

A good **scientific explanation** will provide reasons for **all** of the data. Many explain some facts, but not all of them.

Facts and explanations could be used to evaluate whether an asteroid could destroy the human race.

Unlike the dinosaurs, humans have the technology to detect asteroids, but that doesn't mean we would be able to stop it, or survive an impact.

Module P1 Summary

The Earth

Evidence in rocks show us how the Earth has changed through…
- **erosion**
- **craters** being made
- **mountains forming**.

The Earth must be **older** than its **oldest rocks**.

HT The **oldest rocks** on Earth are about **4000 million years old**.

The **Earth** is made up of…
- the crust
- mantle
- core.

Continental Drift

Wegener's continental drift theory = The continents **fit together** and fossils, rock patterns and mountain ranges **match up**.

Wegener's theory was **rejected** by his peers at the time ➡ Evidence from **seafloor spreading** led to it becoming **accepted**.

Tectonic Plates and Seafloor Spreading

Earth's crust is divided into **tectonic plates**; these plates meet at **plate boundaries**.

Tectonic plates…
- **float** on the **mantle**
- **move apart**, **towards** or **past** each other.

The **mantle** is **fairly solid** below the crust; further down it is **liquid**.

Convection currents in the mantle cause the plates to move; **magma** can rise to the surface and harden, forming new **seafloor**.

HT Plate Tectonics

Earth's **magnetic field** changes polarity every million years and produces **rock stripes** of **alternating polarity**. These occur at **constructive plate boundaries**.

Subduction = The denser **oceanic plate** is forced under the **continental plate**. Occurs at **destructive plate boundaries**.

Mountain ranges form along **colliding** plate boundaries as **sedimentary rock** is forced up by a **collision**.

Plate movement is crucial in the **rock cycle**.

Module P1 Summary

Geohazards

Geohazards...
- are **natural hazards** (e.g. floods)
- can strike without warning so authorities take **precautionary measures**.

The Universe

The **Big Bang** theory explains how the Universe began.

HT The **Solar System** formed 5000 million years ago.

The Solar System began as **dust** and **gas** clouds ➡ **Nuclear fusion** formed the Sun ➡ Smaller masses like **planets, moons, asteroids** and **comets** formed around the Sun.

The Sun's energy comes from **nuclear fusion**: hydrogen atoms **fuse together**.

HT The **nuclei** of hydrogen atoms fuse together during nuclear fusion.

Other galaxies are **moving away** from us.

HT **Hubble's Law** = The speed at which a galaxy is moving away is proportional to its distance.

Space and the Stars

If the distance is great enough, **light speed** can be measured.

HT **Speed of light** = 300 000km/s.

Vast space distances are measured in **light years**.

The distance of a star can be measured using **relative brightness** or **parallax**.

Stars produce radiation.

Stars have a **finite life** and eventually become **red giants** or **red super giants**.

Scientific Explanations

There's no proof of **alien life**, although many scientists think it's possible.

One theory for the extinction of the dinosaurs is that an **asteroid** hit Earth.

A good scientific explanation will provide reasons for **all** the data.

Facts and **explanations** can be used to **evaluate** a theory. A theory needs evaluating by **other scientists** before it's **accepted** — the **Peer review** process.

Module P1 Practice Questions

1 The drawing shows the structure of the Earth. Match statements **A, B, C** and **D** with the labels **1–4** on the drawing. Enter the appropriate number in the boxes provided.

A Inner core [2]
B Outer core [3]
C Mantle   [4]
D Crust   [1]

2 Wegener was a scientist who proposed the theory of continental drift. What evidence did Wegener use to support his theory? Tick the three correct options.

A The jigsaw fit of some continents. [✓]
B Other people believed him. [ ]
C Rock patterns are the same on different continents. [✓]
D He used the periodic table. [ ]
E Fossil remains. [✓]

3 a) Fill in the missing word to complete the sentence below:

The Earth's crust is divided into __tectonic__ plates.

b) Name the three ways these plates can move.

i) slide past each other

ii) move towards

iii) move away

4 a) Circle the correct options in the following sentence:

(Convection) / combustion / magma / mantle currents in the **convection** / combustion / magma / **(mantle)** cause **convection** / combustion / **(magma)** / mantle to rise and form new oceanic crust.

b) What is this theory known as?

Seafloor spreading

16

Module P1 Practice Questions

HT

5 How old is the Solar System?

5000 million

6 Fill in the missing words to complete the sentences below:

a) The Solar System began when *gas* and *dust* clouds were pulled together by *gravity* which created intense *heat*.

b) *Nuclear* fusion began and the Sun was born.

c) Smaller masses also formed, which *orbit* the Sun.

7 Name two smaller masses in the Solar System.

a) *comets* **b)** *planets*

8 What are vast distances in space measured in?

light years

9 In what two ways can the distance of a star be measured?

a) *parralax* **b)** *relative brightness*

10 Medium-weight stars like the Sun eventually become a red giant. Fill in the missing words below to complete the next three stages of its life cycle.

a) The red giant's core contracts and it becomes a planetary *nebula*.

b) The star's core cools and contracts further, becoming a ~~cool~~ *white* dwarf.

c) It cools further to become a ~~white~~ *black* dwarf.

11 Fill in the missing words to complete the sentence below:

If a source of light is moving away from us, the ~~speed~~ *wavelengths* of light are ~~slower~~ *longer* than if the source was stationary.

12 Name a theory of how the Universe began.

Big bang

17

Radiation and Life

The Electromagnetic Spectrum

The **electromagnetic spectrum** is a family of seven radiations, including **visible light**.

A **beam** of electromagnetic radiation contains '**packets**' of energy called **photons**.

Different radiations contain photons that carry **different amounts** of energy.

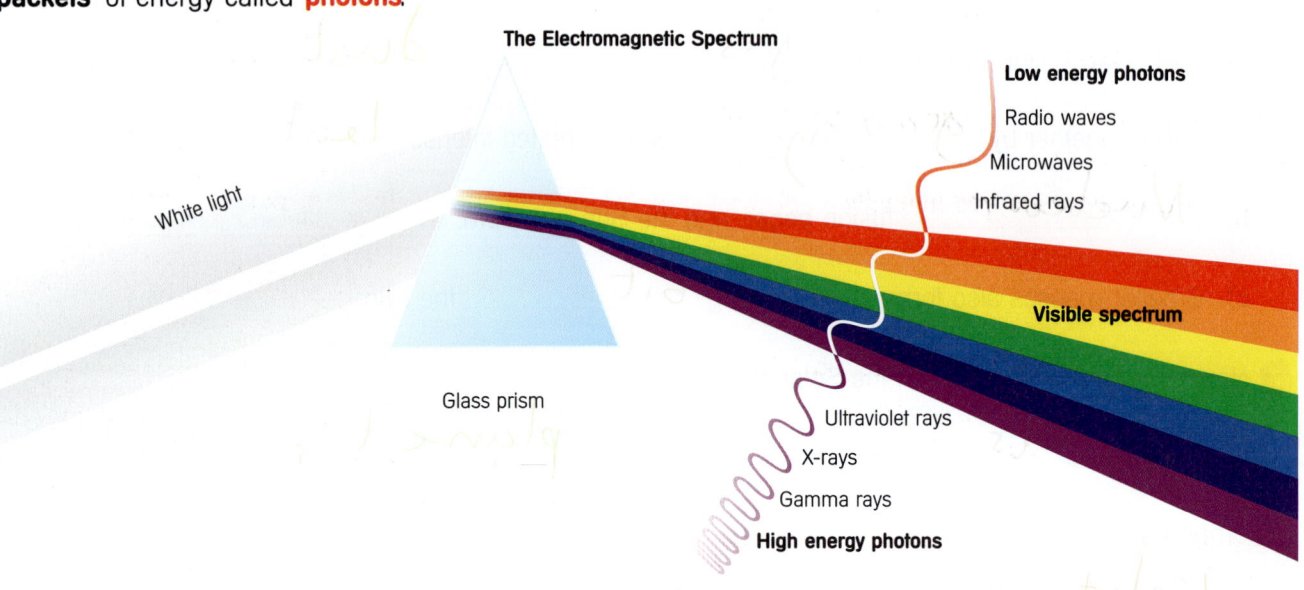

Transmitting Radiation

The general model of radiation shows how energy travels from a **source** which **emits** radiation, to a **detector** which **absorbs** radiation.

On the journey from **emitter** to **detector**, materials can **transmit**, **reflect** or **absorb** radiation.

For example, clouds absorb and reflect the Sun's energy, so on a cloudy day we receive less light than on a clearer day.

Emitter	Type of Waves	Detector
TV transmitter	Radio waves	TV aerial
Mobile phone mast	Microwaves	Mobile phones
The Sun	Light	The eye
Remote control	Infrared waves	Television
Some stars (e.g. supernova)	Gamma rays	Gamma ray telescope
X-ray machine	X-rays	Photographic plate

Intensity and Heat

The **intensity** of electromagnetic radiation is the energy arriving at a **surface per second**.

Intensity depends on the number of photons delivered per second and the amount of energy each packet contains, i.e. the photon energy.

The intensity of a beam **decreases** with distance, so the further from a source you are, the lower the intensity.

When a material absorbs radiation, heat is created. The amount of heat depends on its intensity.

Key Words

Electromagnetic spectrum • Ion • Photon

Radiation and Life

HT Intensity and Heat

The decrease in intensity is due to three factors:
- Photons **spread out** as they travel.
- Some photons are **absorbed** by particles in the substances they pass through.
- Some photons are **reflected** and **scattered** by other particles.

These factors **combine** to reduce the number of photons arriving per second at a detector. This results in a **lower measured intensity**.

When a material absorbs radiation, heat is created; the amount of heat depends on its intensity.

The amount of heat created depends on…
- the **intensity** of the radiation beam
- the **duration** of the exposure.

Ionising Radiation

Ionising radiation (electromagnetic radiation with a high photon energy) can break molecules into bits called **ions**. **Ultraviolet** radiation, **X-rays** and **gamma rays** are examples of ionising radiation.

HT Ions are **very reactive** and can easily take part in other chemical reactions.

Cell Damage

Radiation **damages** living cells in different ways:
- The heating effect can damage the skin, e.g. sunburn.
- Ionising radiation can age the skin. It can also **mutate** DNA, which can lead to cancer.
- Different amounts of exposure can cause different effects, e.g. high intensity ionising radiation can destroy cells, leading to **radiation poisoning**.

Microwaves can heat materials by causing the water particles to vibrate. There may be a health risk from the low intensity microwaves of mobile phones and masts, but this is disputed. One study found no link from short-term use but other studies have found some correlation.

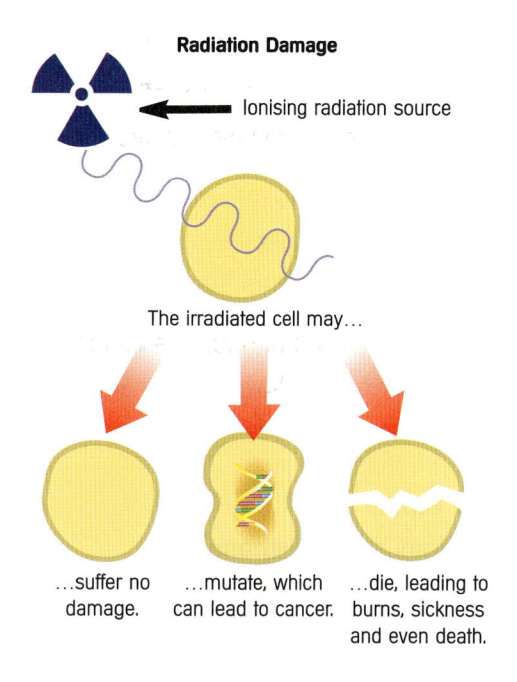

Radiation Damage

The irradiated cell may…
- …suffer no damage.
- …mutate, which can lead to cancer.
- …die, leading to burns, sickness and even death.

19

Radiation and Life

Radiation Protection

Microwave ovens have a metal case and a wire screen in the door to absorb microwaves and stop too much radiation escaping.

Other **physical barriers** are used to protect people:
- X-ray technicians use **lead screens**.
- Sunscreens and clothing can absorb ultraviolet radiation to help prevent skin cancer.
- Nuclear reactors are encased in thick lead and concrete.

People going into areas of high radiation must wear a **radiation suit** as a shield.

The Sun and the Ozone Layer

Light radiation from the Sun…
- warms the Earth's surface
- is used by plants for **photosynthesis**.

Photosynthesis **counteracts** respiration – it removes carbon dioxide and adds oxygen.

The **ozone layer** is a thin layer of gas in the Earth's upper atmosphere. It absorbs some of the Sun's ultraviolet radiation before it reaches Earth.

Without the ozone layer, the amount of radiation reaching Earth would be **very harmful**. Living organisms, especially animals, would suffer cell damage.

> **HT** The energy from ultraviolet radiation causes chemical changes in the upper atmosphere when it's absorbed by the ozone layer. These changes are **reversible**.

The Greenhouse Effect

The Earth emits electromagnetic radiation into space. Gases in the atmosphere absorb some of the radiation and this keeps Earth warmer than it would be. This is known as the **greenhouse effect**.

Carbon dioxide (a **greenhouse gas**) makes up a small amount of Earth's atmosphere.

> **HT** Other greenhouse gases include…
> - water vapour
> - trace amounts of **methane**.

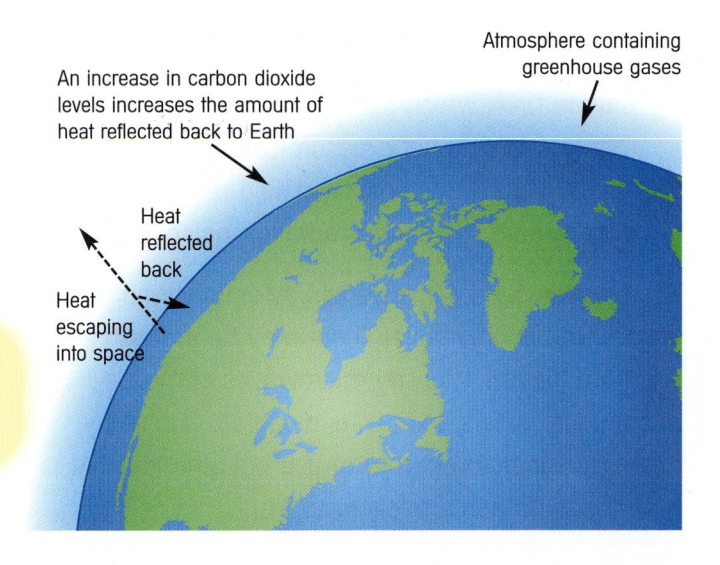

An increase in carbon dioxide levels increases the amount of heat reflected back to Earth

Atmosphere containing greenhouse gases

Heat reflected back

Heat escaping into space

Radiation and Life

The Carbon Cycle

The **carbon cycle** is an example of a balanced system.

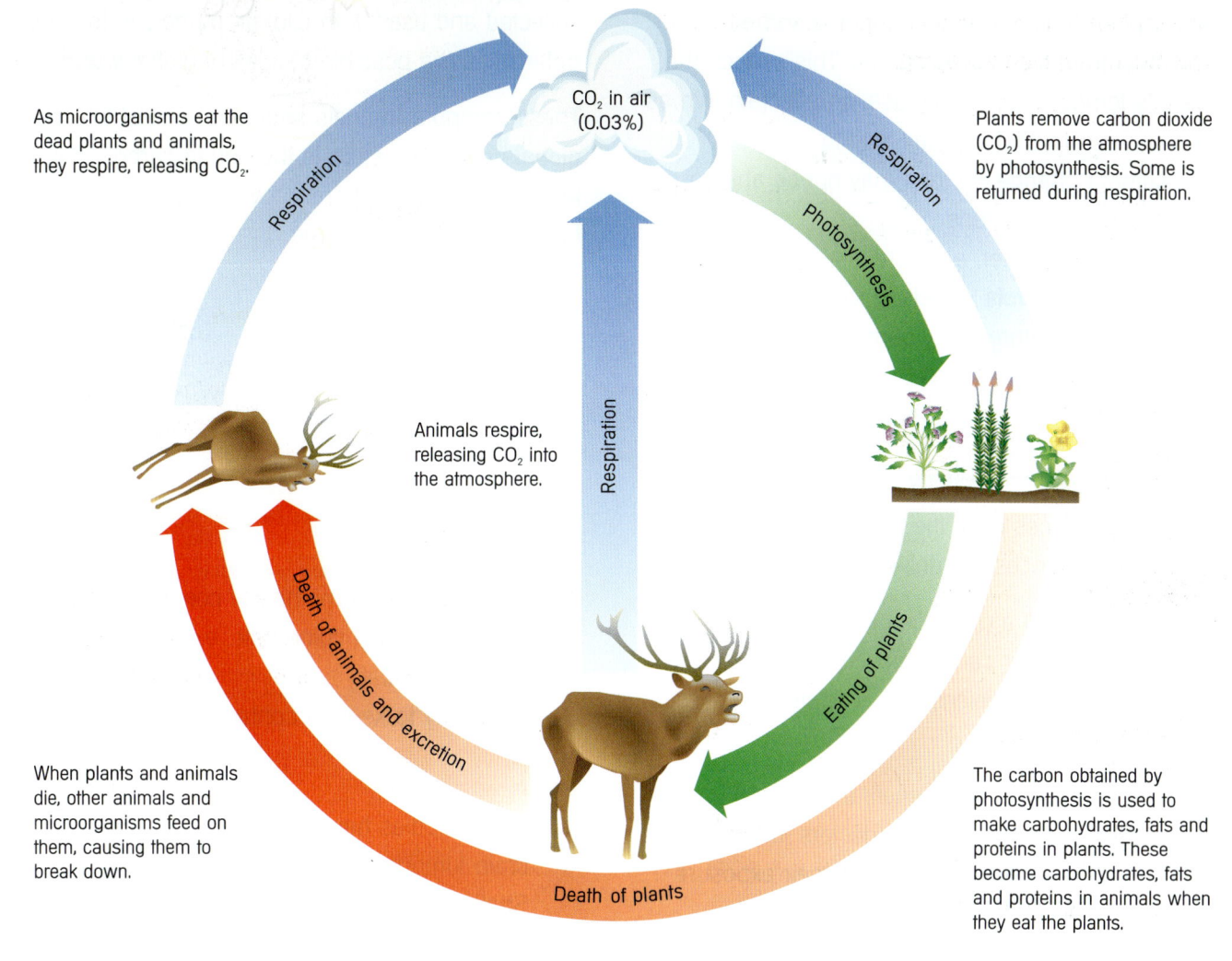

As microorganisms eat the dead plants and animals, they respire, releasing CO_2.

CO_2 in air (0.03%)

Plants remove carbon dioxide (CO_2) from the atmosphere by photosynthesis. Some is returned during respiration.

Respiration

Respiration

Photosynthesis

Animals respire, releasing CO_2 into the atmosphere.

Respiration

Eating of plants

Death of animals and excretion

When plants and animals die, other animals and microorganisms feed on them, causing them to break down.

Death of plants

The carbon obtained by photosynthesis is used to make carbohydrates, fats and proteins in plants. These become carbohydrates, fats and proteins in animals when they eat the plants.

Using the Carbon Cycle

The carbon cycle can be used to explain several points:

- Carbon dioxide (CO_2) levels in the Earth's atmosphere remained roughly **constant** for thousands of years because it was constantly being **recycled** by plants and animals.
- **Decomposers** are important microorganisms that break down dead material and release CO_2.
- CO_2 levels in the atmosphere have been steadily increasing, largely due to human activity, e.g. burning **fossil fuels** and **deforestation**.
- Burning fossil fuels releases carbon that was removed from the atmosphere millions of years ago and had been 'locked up' ever since.
- Burning forests not only release carbon, but also reduces the number of plants removing CO_2 from the atmosphere.

Key Words

Carbon cycle • Decomposer • Deforestation • Greenhouse effect • Ozone layer • Photosynthesis

Radiation and Life

Global Warming

The increase in greenhouse gases in the Earth's atmosphere means the amount of absorbed radiation from the Sun increases. This causes the Earth's temperature to increase, an effect known as **global warming**, which may lead to…

- **climate change** – crops may not be able to grow in some areas
- **extreme weather**, e.g. hurricanes
- **rising sea levels** – melting ice caps and higher sea temperatures may cause sea levels to rise, flooding low-lying land.

HT Data about the Earth's changing temperature is collected and used with climate models to look for **patterns** in the possible causes of global **warming**.

These computer models show that one of the main global warming factors is the rise in carbon dioxide levels in the atmosphere, providing evidence that human activity is to blame.

Risk and Benefit

All new advances have the potential for **risk**. Radiation advances are unlikely to be risk-free.

For example, until a correlation between mobile phones and cancer can be proved, people need to make their own decisions and evaluate the risks against the **benefits**.

Another example of risk, benefit and control is X-rays. Although X-rays allow doctors to make a much more **accurate** diagnosis, their exposure times have to be controlled.

X-ray radiation can destroy cancerous cells, but it can harm healthy cells too.

HT A study may show a **correlation** (link) between a **factor** and an **outcome**. But this **doesn't** mean that the factor will always **cause** the outcome.

For example, there may be a link between mobile phones (factor) and cancer (outcome). But, using a mobile phone will not always lead to cancer.

Some people say it's better to take **precautionary measures**, e.g. limit usage, especially for young people.

Benefits of Mobile Phones
- Easy convenient method of communication, especially when vulnerable, e.g. if your car breaks down.
- Easy way to keep in contact.

Risks of Mobile Phones
- Some studies have linked mobile phones to brain tumours.
- Studies are still being carried out and the long-term effects aren't known.

Risk Reduction
- Limit usage to emergencies and texting.
- Use a hands-free kit.
- Avoid using when the signal's low.

Radiation and Life

Weighing the Risks

In weighing up a risk it's important to consider the chance of the **outcome** and any **consequences**. Although a risk may seem low, the outcome could be very serious.

For example, although there's evidence that prolonged exposure to ultraviolet light increases the risk of skin cancer, many people still sunbathe. Some reasons could be that…

- sunlight is needed for good health and is a source of vitamin D
- sunlight can help prevent SAD (seasonal affective disorder) and skin conditions such as eczema
- people think a tan looks healthy or attractive
- people think it won't happen to them.

HT The ALARA Principle

Actual risk is a **scientific measure** of the dangers of something. **Perceived risk** is how dangerous people think it is.

These **values** can be very different. Factors that affect perceived risk include…

- media coverage and personal bias
- social influence, e.g. opinions of family.

The **ALARA** (**As Low As Reasonably Achievable**) principle is used as a guideline for **risk management**. It states that measures should be taken to make the risks as small as possible, whilst still providing the **benefits** and taking into account **social**, **economic** and **practical implications**. For example, this is used in radiology units to protect staff, and to control the dose of radiation given in each treatment.

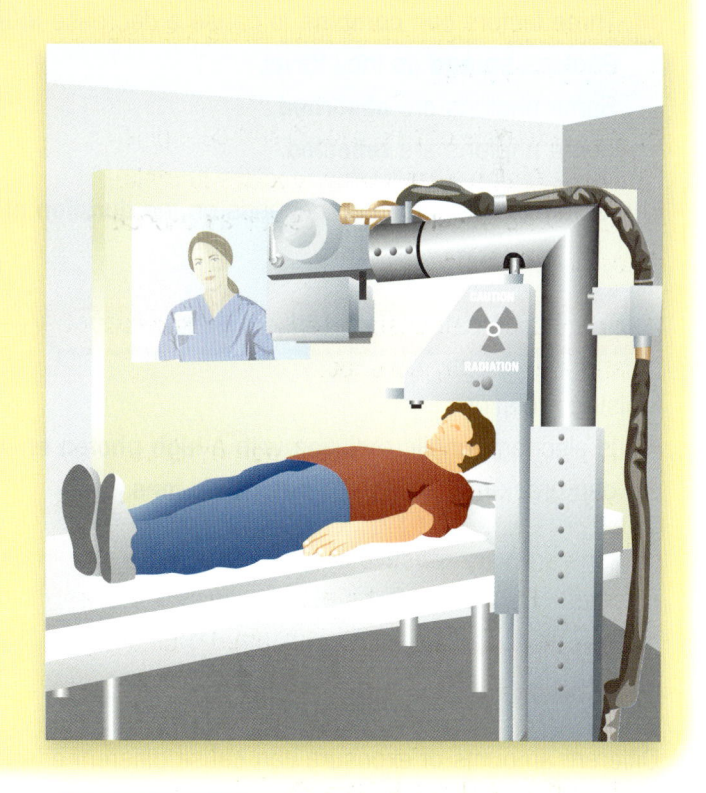

Key Words
ALARA • Global warming • Risk

Module P2 Summary

The Electromagnetic Spectrum

The **electromagnetic spectrum** = Seven radiations, including **visible light**.

A **beam** of electromagnetic radiation contains **photons**.

Different radiations contain photons that carry **different amounts** of **energy**.

Transmitting Radiation

Emitter (a source of radiation) ➡ **Detector** (absorbs radiation)

Radiation energy travels from an emitter to a detector – materials can **transmit**, **reflect** or **absorb** this radiation.

Intensity and Heat

Intensity of **electromagnetic radiation** = Energy arriving at a **surface per second**.

Intensity depends on the **number of photons** delivered **per second** and the **amount of photon energy**.

The intensity of a beam **decreases** with distance. The further from a source you are, the **lower** the intensity.

Heat is created when a material **absorbs** radiation – the **amount** of heat depends on the intensity.

> **HT** Three factors can **combine** to cause a decrease in intensity:
> - Photons **spread** as they travel.
> - Some photons are **absorbed**.
> - Some photons are **reflected**.
>
> The amount of heat created depends on the **duration** of **exposure**.

Ionising Radiation

Ionising radiation…
- is electromagnetic radiation with a **high photon energy**
- can break molecules into **bits** called **ions**.

> **HT** Ions are **very reactive** and can easily take part in other reactions.

Ionising Radiation and Health

Different amounts of exposure can cause different effects. **High intensity** ionising radiation can destroy cells leading to **radiation poisoning**.

There may be a **health risk** from microwaves in mobile phone use.

Physical barriers, e.g. radiation suits, protect people in areas of high radiation.

Module P2 Summary

The Sun and the Ozone Layer

Light radiation from the **Sun** warms Earth and is used in **photosynthesis**.

The **ozone layer** absorbs **ultraviolet radiation** before it reaches Earth ➡ Without this layer the radiation would be very **harmful**.

The Greenhouse Effect

Greenhouse effect = Gases in the atmosphere absorb radiation and keep the Earth warmer than it would be.

Carbon dioxide = A **greenhouse gas**.

HT Other greenhouse gases include **water vapour** and **methane**.

Global Warming

Global warming causes **climate change**, **extreme weather** and **rising sea levels**.

The **increase** in greenhouse gases in the atmosphere means the temperature of the Earth **increases**.

HT Computer climate models use data to look for patterns to find the cause of global warming.

The rise in carbon dioxide levels has been shown to be a factor in global warming ➡ Human activity is to blame.

The Carbon Cycle

The **carbon cycle** is a balanced system:
1. **Plants** remove **carbon dioxide** from the atmosphere.
2. Carbon from photosynthesis makes **carbohydrates**, **fats** and **proteins**.
3. Animals and microorganisms feed on dead animals to **break them down**.
4. Microorganisms and animals **respire**, releasing carbon dioxide.

Carbon dioxide levels once remained constant – they were **recycled** by plants and animals. Levels have risen because of **human activity**, e.g. deforestation.

Risk and Benefit

Radiation advances are unlikely to be **risk-free**. Until a correlation is **proven**, people need to assess the **risks** against the **benefits**.

HT ALARA = As Low As Reasonably Achievable

ALARA – a guideline for **risk management**.

Module P2 Practice Questions

1 Circle the correct options in the following sentences:

a) A **beam** / photon / packet / ion of electromagnetic radiation contains beams / photons / **packets** / ions of energy called beams / **photons** / packets / ions.

b) Radiation energy travels from a source known as the detector / photon / **emitter** / spectrum to a **detector** / photon / emitter / spectrum.

2 a) Fill in the missing words to complete the sentence below:

Intensity depends on the number of _photons_ delivered per _second_ and the amount of _energy_ each _photon_ contains.

b) Which of the following statements is true? Tick the correct option.

A The intensity of a beam of light decreases with distance. ✓
B The intensity of a beam of light never changes with distance.
C The intensity of a beam of light energises with distance.
D The intensity of a beam of light increases with distance.

HT c) Give three factors that combine to reduce the intensity of radiation delivered by the Sun to the Earth's surface.

i) photons reflected

ii) " absorbed

iii) " disperse

3 Name two examples of ionising radiation.

a) gamma

b) x rays

4 Give two examples of how radiation can damage cells.

a) mutation

b) make cells die

Module P2 Practice Questions

5 a) What is the thin layer of gas in the Earth's upper atmosphere called? __ozone__

b) How does this protect the Earth?

absorbs ~~reflects~~ suns energy

c) What would be the consequences if this layer did not exist?

greater intensity of radiations

HT d) Fill in the missing word to complete the sentence below:

Ultraviolet radiation causes __reversable__ chemical changes in the upper atmosphere.

6 a) Why did carbon dioxide levels remain constant for thousands of years?

plants took it out of atmosphere

b) Give two reasons why carbon dioxide levels have now started increasing.

i) deforestation

ii) fossil fuels

7 Name three consequences of global warming, and give an example for each.

a) Consequence: Climate Change   Example: No crops

b) Consequence: Rising sea   Example: Flooding

c) Consequence: Weather   Example: Hurricane

HT

8 a) What do the letters ALARA stand for?

As low as reasonable achievable

b) Explain the ALARA principle.

keep risk as low as can be achieved

Radioactive Materials

Atoms and Elements

All **elements** are made of **atoms**; each element contains only one type of atom. All atoms contain a **nucleus** and **electrons**.

The nucleus is made from **protons** and **neutrons**. Hydrogen (the lightest element) is the one exception; it has no neutrons, just one proton and one electron.

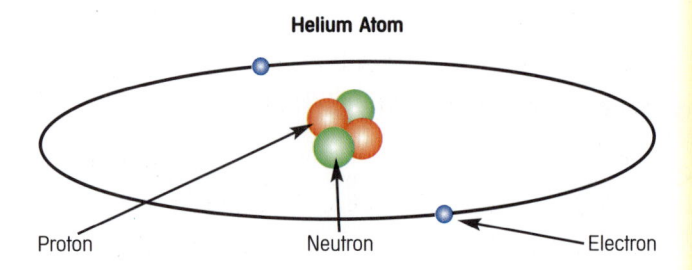

Helium Atom

Proton — Neutron — Electron

Radioactive elements emit ionising radiation all the time. Neither chemical reactions nor physical processes (e.g. smelting) can change the radioactive behaviour of a substance.

HT Every atom of a **particular element** always has the same number of protons. (If it contained a different number of protons it would be a different element.) For example…

- hydrogen atoms have 1 proton
- helium atoms have 2 protons
- oxygen atoms have 8 protons.

But, some atoms of the same element can have **different numbers of neutrons** – these are **isotopes**. For example, there are three isotopes of oxygen:

Oxygen-16 has 8 neutrons

Oxygen-17 has 9 neutrons

Oxygen-18 has 10 neutrons.

N.B. All three of these isotopes have 8 protons.

Ionising Radiation

Radioactive materials can give out three types of ionising radiation:

- **Alpha**
- **Beta**
- **Gamma**.

Different radioactive materials will give out any one, or a combination, of these radiations.

The different types of radiation have different penetrating powers.

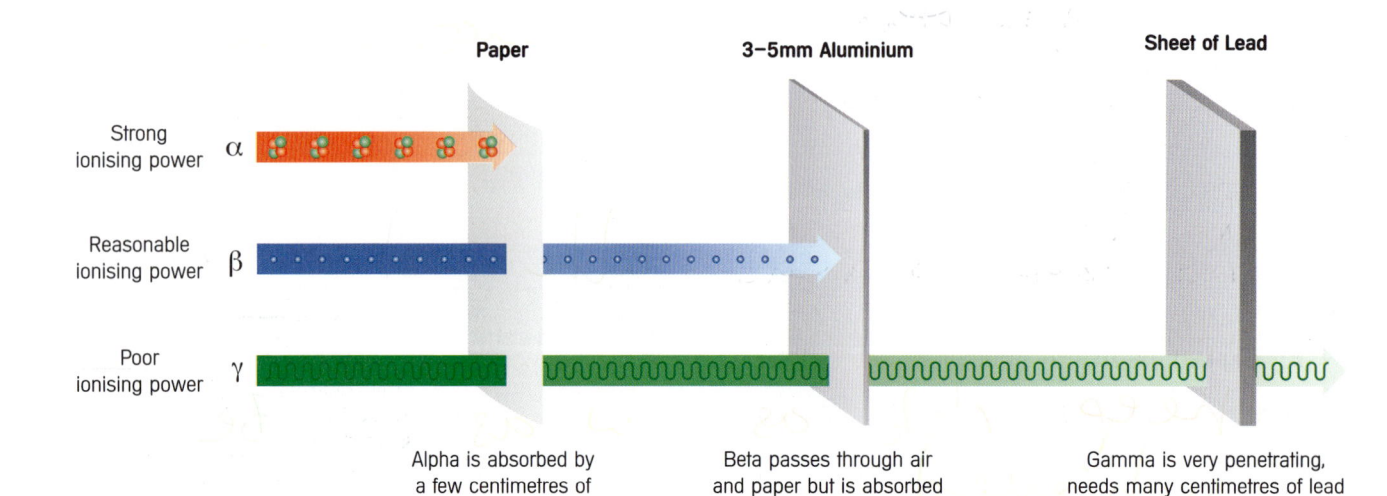

Paper — 3–5mm Aluminium — Sheet of Lead

Strong ionising power α

Reasonable ionising power β

Poor ionising power γ

Alpha is absorbed by a few centimetres of air or a thin sheet of paper.

Beta passes through air and paper but is absorbed by a few millimetres of aluminium.

Gamma is very penetrating, needs many centimetres of lead or many metres of concrete to absorb most of it.

Radioactive Materials

Radioactive Decay

Ionising radiation is emitted when the nucleus of an unstable atom decays. The type of **radioactive decay** depends on why the nucleus is unstable; the process of decay helps the atom become more **stable**. During decay the number of protons may change. If this happens the element changes to another type.

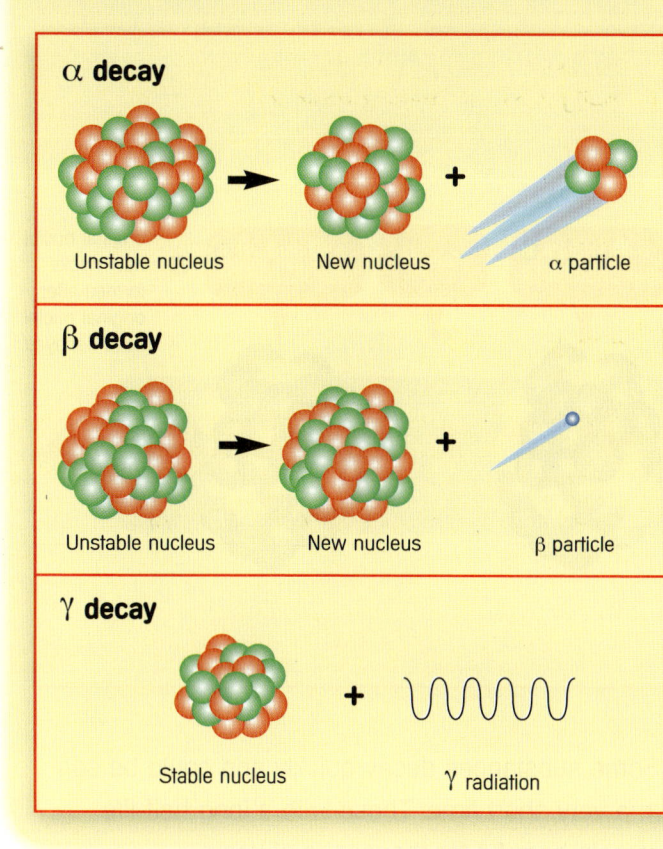

α decay	The original atom decays by ejecting an **alpha** (α) **particle** from the nucleus. This particle is a **helium nucleus**: a particle made of two protons and two neutrons. With **alpha decay** a new atom is formed. This new atom has two protons and two neutrons fewer than the original.
β decay	The original atom decays by changing a neutron into a proton and an electron. This high energy electron, which is now ejected from the nucleus, is a **beta** (β) **particle**. With **beta decay** a new atom is formed. This new atom has one more proton and one less neutron than the original.
γ decay	After α or β decay, a nucleus sometimes contains surplus energy. It emits this as **gamma** radiation (very high frequency electromagnetic radiation). During gamma decay, only energy is emitted. This decay doesn't change the type of atom.

Background Radiation

Radioactive elements are found naturally in the environment and contribute to **background radiation**. Nothing can stop us being **irradiated** and **contaminated** by background radiation, but generally the levels are so low it's nothing to worry about. However, there's a **correlation** between certain cancers and living in particular areas, especially among people who have lived in granite buildings for many years.

Sources of Background Radiation

- **Radon gas** – Released at surface of ground from uranium in rocks and soil.
- **From food**
- **γ rays** – From rocks, soil and building materials.
- **Cosmic rays** – From outer space and the Sun.
- **Medical** – Mainly X-rays.
- **Nuclear industry**

Key Words

Atom • Alpha • Beta • Electron • Element • Gamma • Isotopes • Neutron • Nucleus • Proton

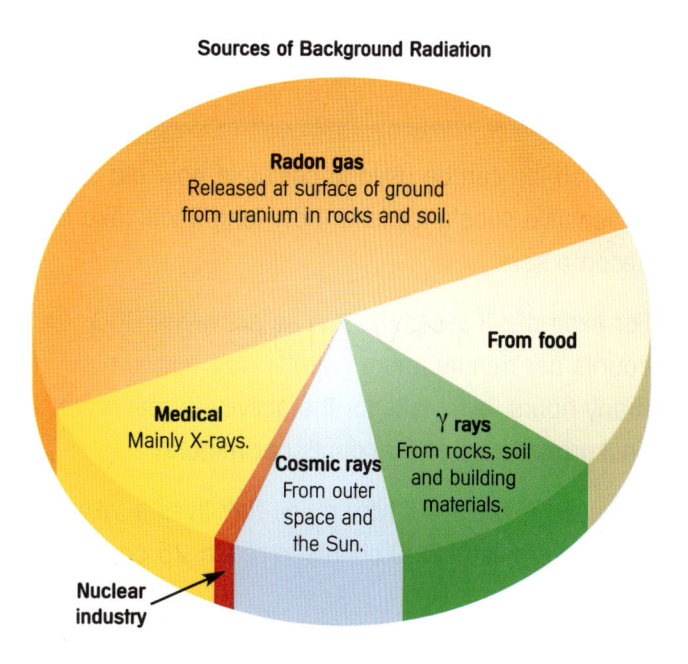

Radioactive Materials

Half-life

As a radioactive atom decays, its activity drops. This means that its radioactivity decreases over time.

The **half-life** of a substance is the time it takes for its radioactivity to halve.

Different substances have different half-lives, ranging from a few seconds to thousands of years.

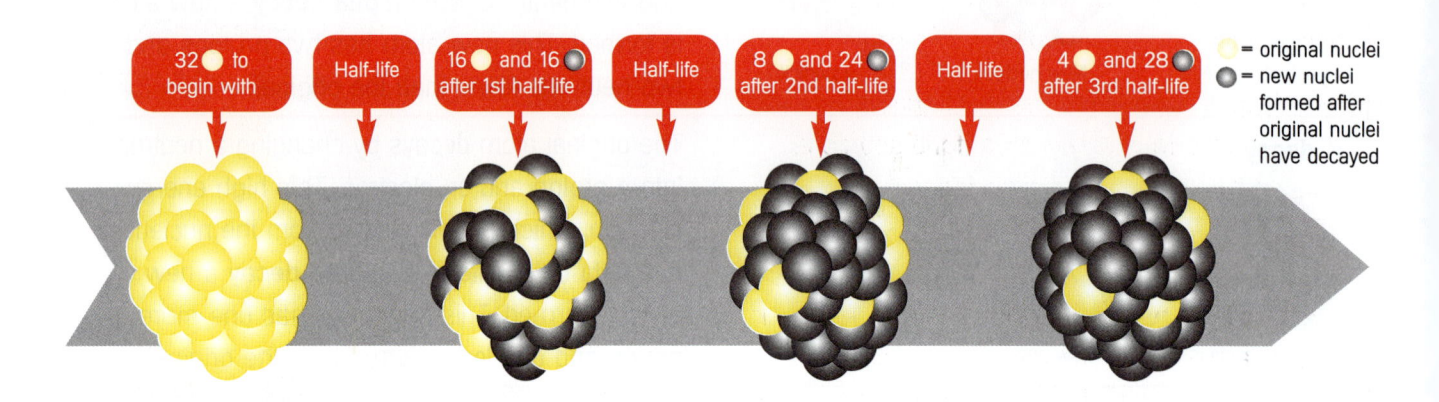

- 32 to begin with
- 16 and 16 after 1st half-life
- 8 and 24 after 2nd half-life
- 4 and 28 after 3rd half-life

○ = original nuclei
● = new nuclei formed after original nuclei have decayed

Half-life and Safety

A substance is considered safe once its activity drops to the same level as background radiation. This is a dose of around 2 millisieverts per year or 25 counts per minute with a standard detector.

Some substances decay quickly and could be safe in a very short time. Those with a long half-life remain harmful for thousands of years.

HT Half-life Calculations

The half-life can be used to calculate how old a radioactive substance is, or how long it will take to become safe.

For example, if a sample has an activity of 800 counts per minute and a half-life of 2 hours, how many hours will it take for the activity to reach the background rate of 25 counts per minute?

We need to work out how many half-lives it takes for the sample of 800 counts to reach 25 counts.

① $\frac{800}{2}$ = 400   ② $\frac{400}{2}$ = 200   ③ $\frac{200}{2}$ = 100   ④ $\frac{100}{2}$ = 50   ⑤ $\frac{50}{2}$ = 25

It takes 5 half-lives to reach a count of 25, and each half-life takes 2 hours.

So, it takes 5 x 2 hours = 10 hours.

Radioactive Materials

Dangers of Radiation

Ionising radiation can break molecules into ions. These ions can harm living cells.

HT Ions are **very reactive** and can take part in other chemical reactions.

Many jobs involve using radioactive materials (e.g. the nuclear industry, medical physics). People can become **irradiated** or **contaminated** so their exposure needs to be carefully monitored.

Different types of radiation carry different risks:
- **Alpha** is the most dangerous if the source is **inside the body**; all the radiation will be absorbed by cells in the body.
- **Beta** is the most dangerous if the source is **outside the body**. Unlike alpha, it can penetrate the outer layer of skin and damage internal organs.
- **Gamma** can cause harm if it's absorbed by the cells, but it is weakly ionising and can pass straight through the body causing no damage at all.

The **sievert** is a measure of a radiation dose's potential to harm a person. It's based on both the type and the amount of radiation absorbed.

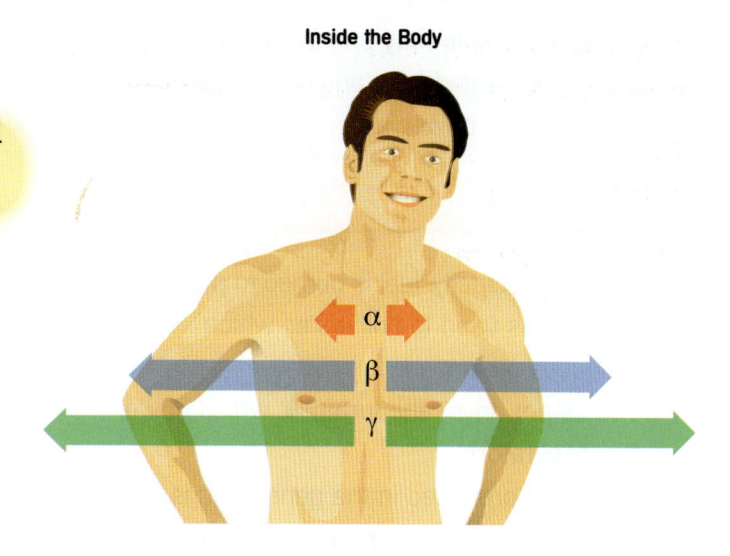

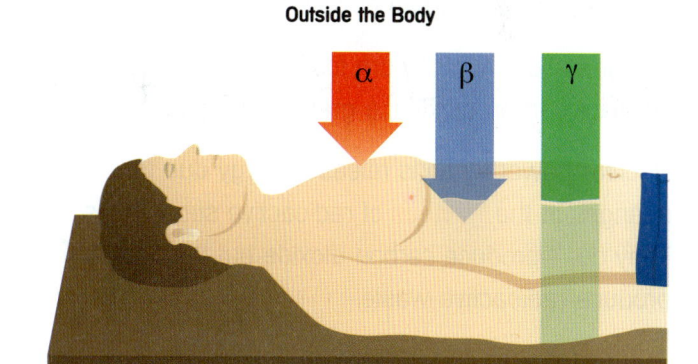

Uses of Radiation

Although using ionising radiation can be dangerous, there are many beneficial uses.

High-energy gamma rays in **cancer treatment** can destroy cancer cells but can damage healthy cells too. The radiation has to be carefully targeted from different angles to minimise the damage.

In radiation treatment for cancer there is a danger of damage to healthy cells – doctors need to carefully weigh the risks against the benefits before going ahead.

HT Risks must be assessed and the **ALARA** principle applied (see page 23).

Radiation is also used to **sterilise surgical instruments** and to **sterilise food**. This kills bacteria.

HT The **precautionary principle** is applied if the risks are unknown, e.g. only a few foods are allowed radiation treatment and they must carry a label stating this. The priority is to protect the public.

Key Words

ALARA • Alpha • Beta • Gamma • Half-life • Irradiated • Precautionary principle

Radioactive Materials

Electricity

Electricity is a **secondary** energy source. This means it's generated from another energy source, e.g. coal, nuclear power, etc.

Electricity is a very useful energy source as it can be easily transmitted over long distances and used in many ways.

Generating Electricity

To generate electricity, fuel is burned to produce heat:
1. The heat is used to boil water, which produces **steam**.
2. The steam drives the **turbines**, which power the **generators**.
3. Electricity produced in the generators is sent to a **transformer** and then to the National Grid, from where you can access it in your home.

Power stations which burn fossil fuels like coal produce carbon dioxide, a greenhouse gas.

Nuclear power stations release energy due to changes in the **nucleus** of radioactive substances. They don't produce carbon dioxide but they do produce radioactive waste.

Nuclear waste is categorised into three types:
- **High-level waste** (HLW) — very radioactive waste that has to be stored carefully. Fortunately, only small amounts are produced and it doesn't remain radioactive for long, so it's put into short-term storage.
- **Intermediate-level waste** (ILW) — not as radioactive as HLW but it remains radioactive for thousands of years. Increasing amounts are produced; deciding how to store it is a problem. At the moment most ILW is mixed with concrete and stored in big containers, but this isn't a permanent solution.
- **Low-level waste** (LLW) — only slightly radioactive waste that is sealed and placed in landfills.

Electricity from Fossil Fuels

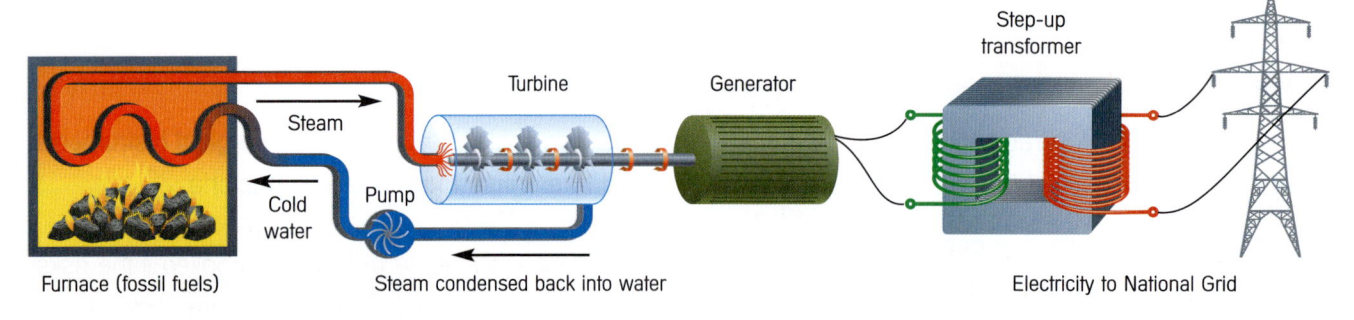

Electricity from Nuclear Fuels

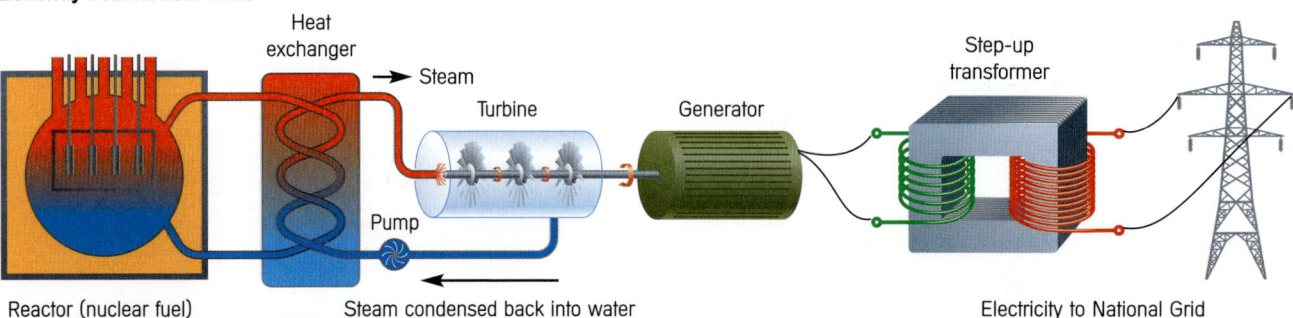

Radioactive Materials

Sankey Diagrams

Energy is lost at every stage of the process of electricity generation.

Sankey diagrams can be used to show the generation and distribution of electricity, including the efficiency of **energy transfers**.

The Sankey diagram shows that from the energy put into the power station, almost half is lost to the surroundings (mostly as heat) before the electricity even reaches the home.

Further energy is lost during energy transfers in the home when the electricity is used.

A Sankey Diagram

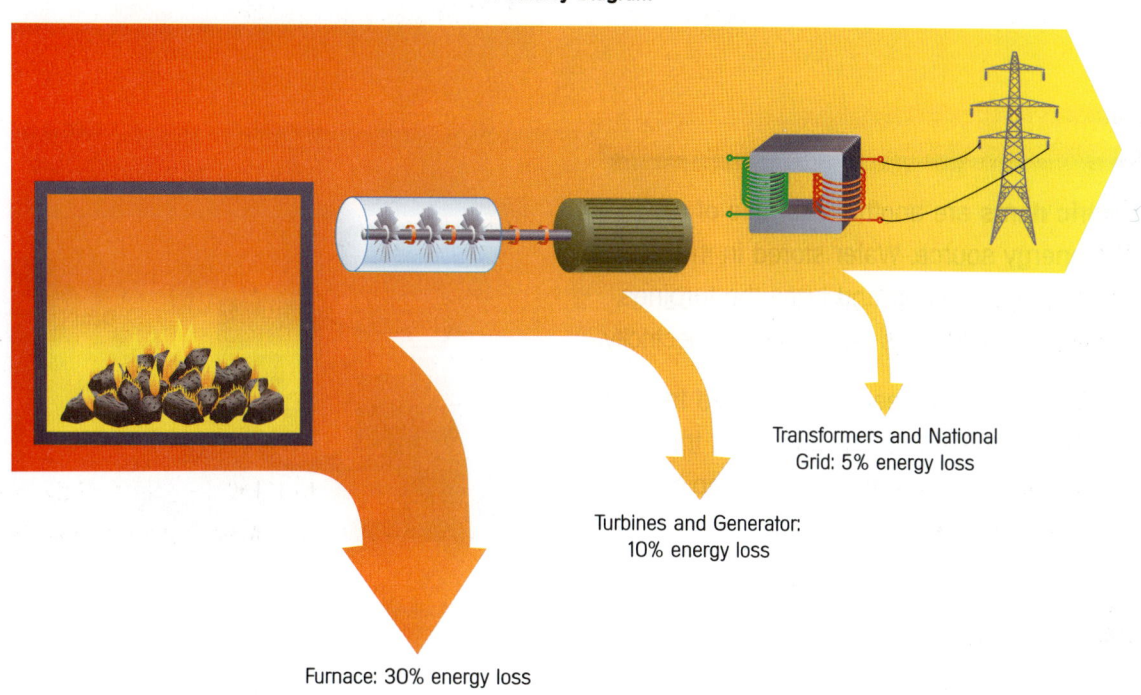

Transformers and National Grid: 5% energy loss

Turbines and Generator: 10% energy loss

Furnace: 30% energy loss

Renewable Energy

Conventional energy supplies are running out and both nuclear and fossil fuels cause environmental damage. This means that **alternative energy sources** are becoming more important.

Alternative ways to generate electricity include **wind**, **water** and **solar** power. These are **renewable energy** sources so will not run out like fossil fuels.

Key Words
Energy transfer • Nuclear waste • Nucleus • Renewable

Radioactive Materials

Wind Turbines

An example of a **renewable energy** source is **wind turbines**. The force of the wind turns the blades of the wind turbine, which provides power to a generator. The amount of electricity produced is small. It would need hundreds of wind turbines to replace a conventional power station. However, once built they provide **free energy**, as long as the wind is blowing.

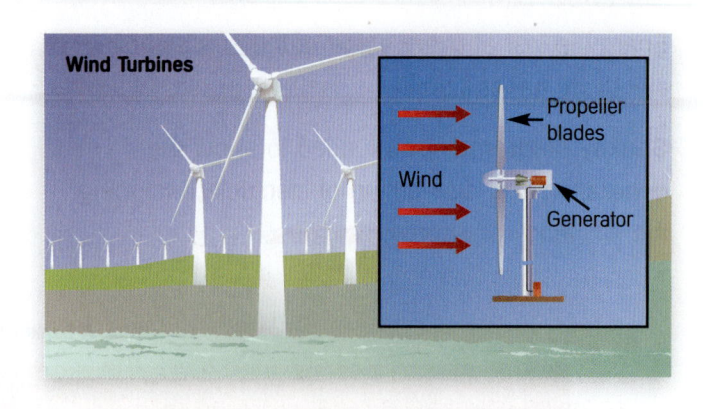

Hydroelectric Dam

Hydroelectric dams are another example of a renewable energy source. Water stored in the **reservoir** flows down pipes and turns the turbines, which powers the generators and produces electricity.

Large areas of land may need to be flooded to build **hydroelectric stations**. However, once built they provide large amounts of reliable, fairly cheap energy.

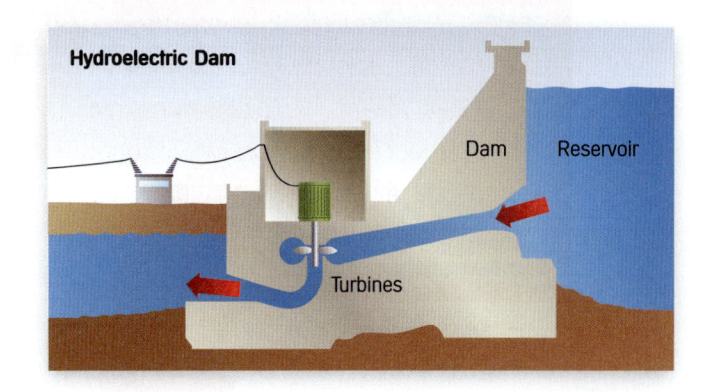

Comparing Benefits

When comparing energy sources for generating electricity, the factors used to assess which source is the most favourable are **efficiency**, **cost** and **environmental damage**.

HT **Power output** and **lifetime** (how long it lasts for) can also be assessed when comparing energy sources.

Key Words
Chain reaction • Nuclear fission • Nuclear reactor • Uranium

Energy Source	Set-up Cost	Efficiency	Environmental Damage	HT Power Output
Nuclear	Very high	Good	• Nuclear radioactive waste	High
Coal	High	Good	• Mining (construction and any waste) • Acid rain • Greenhouse gases • Emissions from the transport of fuel	High
Wind	Low	Variable daily Needs a lot of wind	• Visual pollution	Low
Hydroelectric	High	Needs rain	• Changes ecosystem through flooding	High

Radioactive Materials

Nuclear Fission

In a **chemical reaction** it is the electrons that cause the change. The elements involved stay the same but join up in different ways.

Nuclear fission takes place in the nucleus of the atom and different elements are formed:

- A **neutron** is absorbed by a large and unstable **uranium** nucleus. This splits the nucleus into two roughly equal-sized smaller nuclei. This releases energy and more neutrons.
- A fission reaction releases far more energy than even the most **exothermic** chemical reactions. Once fission has taken place the neutrons can be absorbed by other nuclei and further fission reactions can take place. This is a **chain reaction**.
- A chain reaction occurs when there's enough **fissile material** to prevent too many neutrons escaping without being absorbed. This is called **critical mass** and ensures every reaction triggers at least one further reaction.

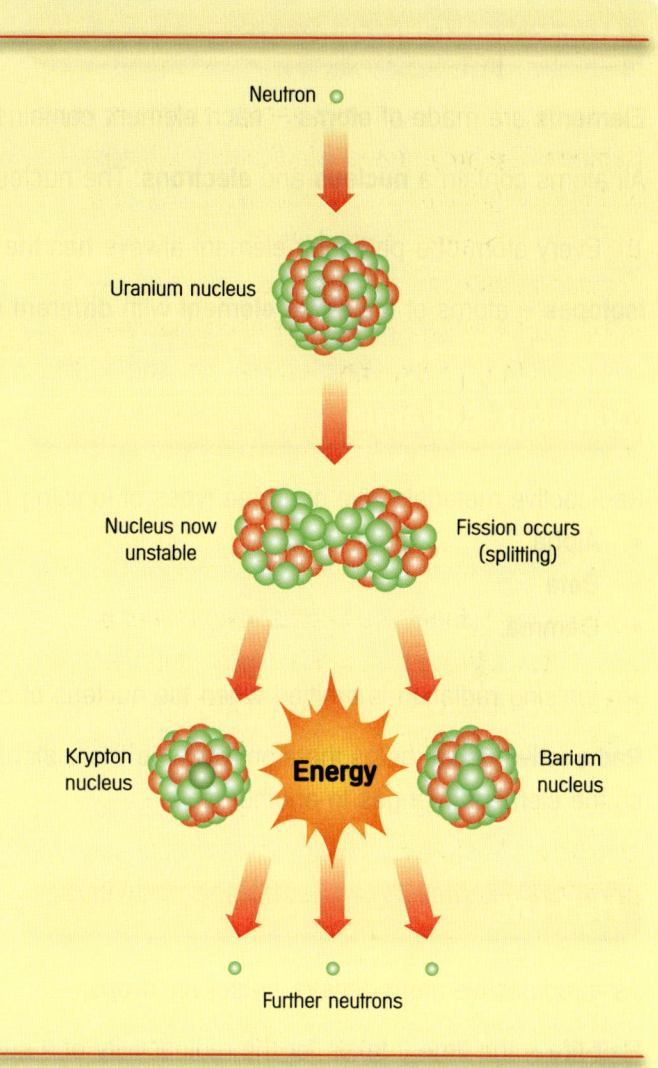

The Nuclear Reactor

Nuclear power stations use fission reactions to generate the heat needed to produce **steam**. The **nuclear reactor** controls the chain reaction so that the energy is steadily released.

Fission occurs in the **fuel rods** and causes them to become very hot.

The **coolant** is a liquid that is pumped through the reactor. The coolant heats up and is then used in the **heat exchanger** to turn water into steam.

Control rods, made of **boron**, absorb neutrons, preventing the chain reaction getting out of control. Moving the control rods in and out of the **reactor core** changes the amount of fission which takes place.

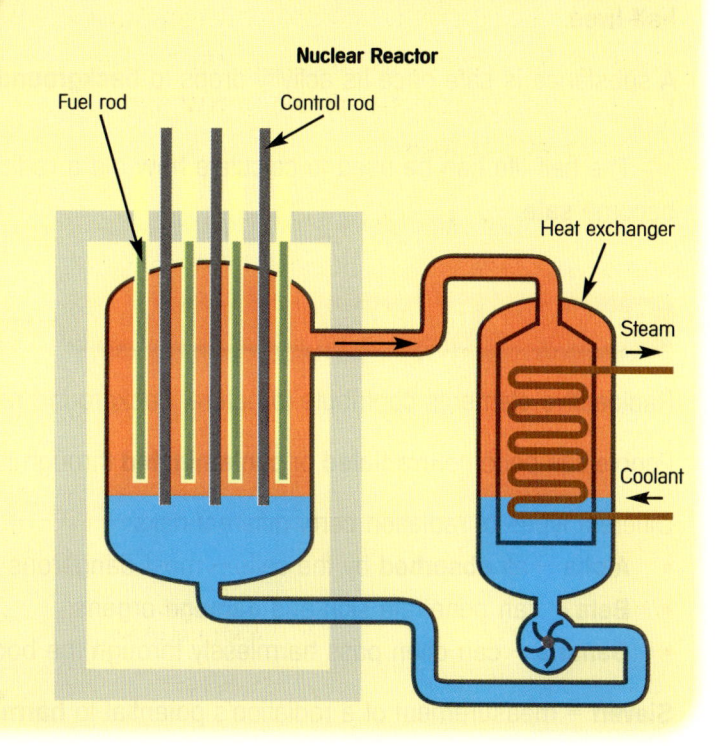

Module P3 Summary

Atoms and Elements

Elements are made of **atoms** – each element contains only one type of atom.

All atoms contain a **nucleus** and **electrons**. The nucleus is made from **protons** and **neutrons**.

> **HT** Every atom of a particular element always has the **same number** of protons.
>
> **Isotopes** = atoms of the **same element** with **different numbers** of neutrons.

Ionising Radiation

Radioactive materials give out three types of ionising radiation:
- **Alpha**
- **Beta**
- **Gamma**.

> **HT** Ionising radiation is emitted when the nucleus of an **unstable atom decays**.
>
> **Radioactive decay** helps the atom become more stable. During decay, the number of protons may change so the element changes to another type.

Half-Life

As a radioactive atom decays, its activity **drops**.

Half-life = the time it takes for the radioactivity of a substance to halve. **Different substances** have **different half-lives**.

A substance is safe once its activity drops to **background radiation levels**.

> **HT** The half-life can be used to calculate how old a radioactive substance is, or how long it will take to become **safe**.

Dangers of Radiation

Radioactive elements contribute to natural background radiation.

People can become **irradiated** or **contaminated** through their job. Their **exposure** needs to be **monitored**.

Different types of radiation carry different risks:
- **Alpha** – all **absorbed** by the cells – most dangerous if the source is inside the body.
- **Beta** – can penetrate skin and **damage** organs.
- **Gamma** – can often pass harmlessly through the body.

Sievert = measurement of a radiation's potential to **harm**.

Module P3 Summary

Uses of Radiation

Ionising radiation is dangerous but has **beneficial uses**:
- Cancer treatment.
- Sterilising surgical instruments.
- Sterilising food.

Electricity

Electricity is a **secondary energy source**.

To produce electricity…
Fuel is burned ➡ Steam drives **turbines** ➡ **Generators** ➡ **Transformer** ➡ **National Grid**.

Power stations produce carbon dioxide, a greenhouse gas.

Nuclear power stations ➡ Release energy from changes in a radioactive substance's nucleus.

Three types of **nuclear waste** are…
- high-level
- intermediate
- low-level.

Energy is lost at **every stage** of electricity generation. **Sankey diagrams** can show this **energy transfer**.

Renewable Energy

Renewable energy source (e.g. **wind turbines** and **hydroelectric dams**). Will not run out like fossil fuels.

Energy sources are compared for **efficiency; cost; environmental damage**.

HT **Power output** and **lifetime** can also be assessed.

Nuclear Fission

Electrons **cause the change** in a chemical reaction; elements stay the same but join up in **different ways**.

Nuclear fission takes place in the **nucleus**:
- A neutron is absorbed by an **unstable** uranium nucleus.
- The nucleus **splits** and releases **energy**.
- A **chain reaction** occurs. **Critical mass**.

Nuclear reactor = controls the chain reaction.

Coolant = heats up and turns water into steam in the **heat exchanger**.

Control rods = made of **boron**, prevent chain reaction getting out of control.

Module P3 Practice Questions

1 a) Name three types of ionising radiation.

i) Alpha

ii) Beta

iii) Gamma

b) Which type of ionising radiation is the most harmful if it gets into the body?

Alpha

c) Name two beneficial uses of ionising radiation.

i) Cancer treatment

ii) Sterilize food

2 State whether the following statements are true or false. Write your answer in the space provided.

a) The radioactivity of a substance increases over time. F

b) An atom's activity drops as it decays. T

c) The half-life of a substance is always less than one thousand years. F

d) Substances all have the same half-life. F

e) A substance is safe once its activity drops to background radiation levels. T

3 Why is electricity described as a secondary energy source?

It's made from another source, nuclear, fossils fuels.

4 a) Name two renewable energy sources.

i) Hydroelectric

ii) Wind

b) Name two advantages of renewable energy.

i) Cleaner, less enviro damage

ii) Renewable resources

Module P3 Practice Questions

5 The diagram shows how electricity is produced from fossil fuels.

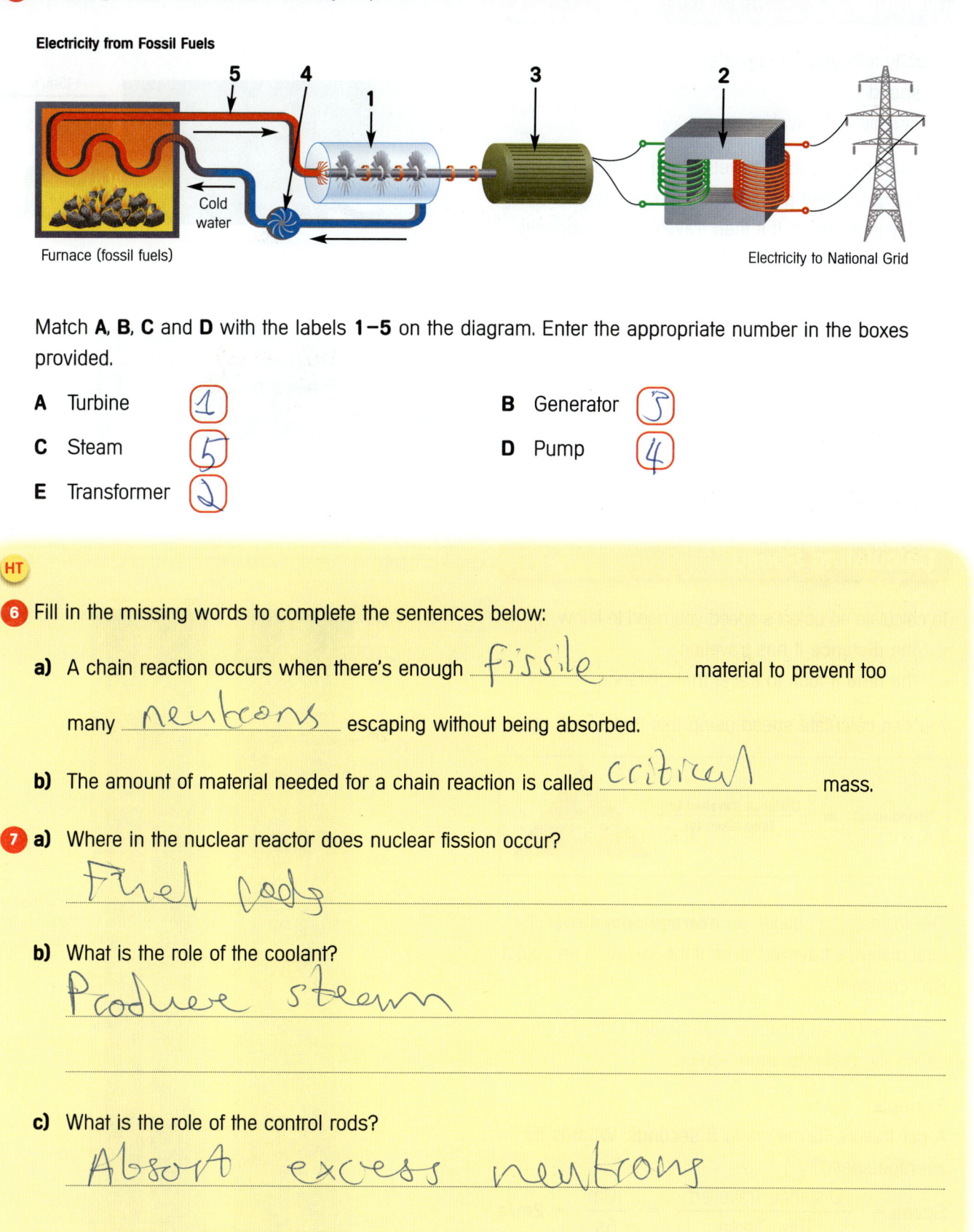

Electricity from Fossil Fuels

Match **A, B, C** and **D** with the labels **1–5** on the diagram. Enter the appropriate number in the boxes provided.

- **A** Turbine — [1]
- **B** Generator — [3]
- **C** Steam — [5]
- **D** Pump — [4]
- **E** Transformer — [2]

HT

6 Fill in the missing words to complete the sentences below:

a) A chain reaction occurs when there's enough __fissile__ material to prevent too many __neutrons__ escaping without being absorbed.

b) The amount of material needed for a chain reaction is called __critical__ mass.

7 a) Where in the nuclear reactor does nuclear fission occur?

__Fuel rods__

b) What is the role of the coolant?

__Produce steam__

c) What is the role of the control rods?

__Absorb excess neutrons__

Explaining Motion

Velocity

Velocity tells you an object's...
- speed
- direction of travel.

For example, if a lorry travels along a straight road at 15m/s (metres per second), in one direction, the velocity is +15m/s. If it then travels in the opposite direction, the velocity is -15m/s.

It doesn't matter which direction is called **positive** or **negative** as long as opposite directions have opposite signs.

This idea is also used when describing **distance**:
- Changes in distance in one direction are described as positive.
- In the opposite direction they're negative.

+15m/s

-15m/s

Calculating Speed

To calculate an object's speed you need to know...
- the **distance** it has travelled
- the **time** it took to travel that distance.

You can calculate speed using this formula:

$$\text{Speed (m/s)} = \frac{\text{Distance travelled (m)}}{\text{Time taken (s)}}$$

$$\frac{d}{s \times t}$$

The formula calculates an **average speed** over the total distance travelled, even if the speed of an object isn't constant.

The speed of an object at a particular point in time is called the **instantaneous speed**.

Example
A car travels 10 metres in 5 seconds. What is its average speed?

$$\text{Speed} = \frac{\text{Distance Travelled}}{\text{Time Taken}} = \frac{10m}{5s} = \mathbf{2m/s}$$

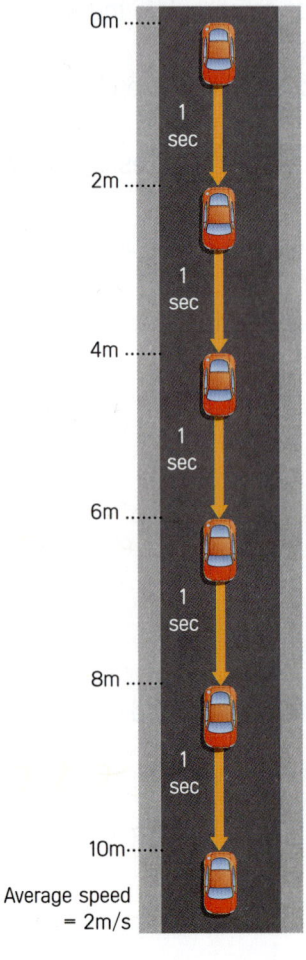

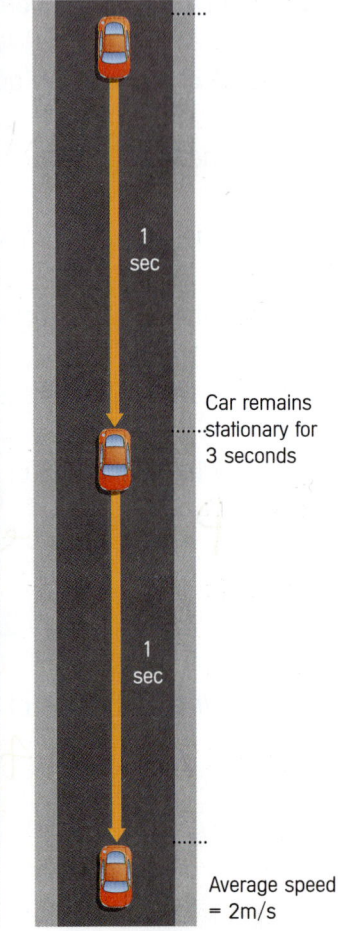

0m, 1 sec, 2m, 1 sec, 4m, 1 sec, 6m, 1 sec, 8m, 1 sec, 10m
Average speed = 2m/s

1 sec, 1 sec, 1 sec
Car remains stationary for 3 seconds
Average speed = 2m/s

Explaining Motion

Distance–Time Graphs

The slope, or **gradient**, of a **distance–time graph** is a measure of the **speed** of the object. The **steeper the slope**, the **greater the speed**.

The graph shows the following:
1. A stationary person standing 15m away from point O.
2. A person moving at a constant speed.
3. A person moving at a greater constant speed.

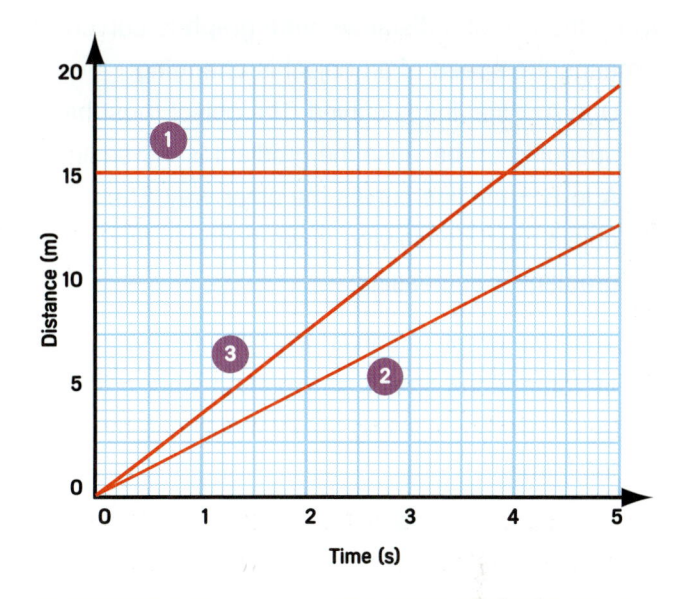

Calculating Speed (HT)

You can calculate the speed of an object by working out the gradient of a distance–time graph:
1. Take any two points on the gradient.
2. Read off the distance travelled between these points.
3. Note the time taken between these points.
4. Divide the distance by the time.

For example:

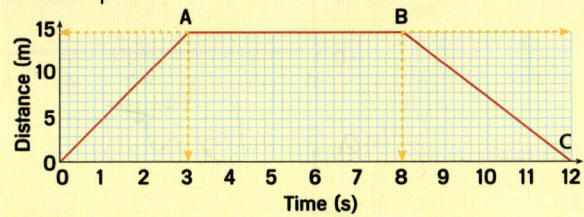

Speed from O to A = $\frac{15m}{3s}$ = **5m/s**

Speed from A to B = $\frac{15m - 15m}{5s}$ = **0m/s**

Speed from B to C = $\frac{15m}{4s}$ = **3.75m/s**

So, the object…
- travelled at 5m/s for 3 seconds
- remained stationary for 5 seconds
- then travelled at 3.75m/s for 4 seconds back to the starting point.

Remember…
- this calculation only works when looking at straight line sections
- the average velocity for this journey is 0 because the object ends up back where it started
- if you're asked to give velocity you need to indicate the direction. If the velocity in the first section is positive, the velocity in the last section will be negative because the object is moving in the opposite direction.

Key Words

Distance–time graph • Gradient • Instantaneous speed • Velocity

Explaining Motion

Curvy Distance–Time Graphs

When the line of a **distance–time graph** is curved, it means the **speed** of an object is **changing**:

- O to A – the line is curved. The object must be speeding up because the gradient is increasing.
- A to B – the line curves the other way. The object must be slowing down because the gradient is decreasing.

Because the graph is curved it's difficult to work out the **instantaneous speed**, but you can work out the average speed by dividing the total distance by the total time.

$$\text{Speed} = \frac{\text{Distance}}{\text{Time}} = \frac{20m}{5s} = 4m/s$$

The dotted line shows the average speed. Where the gradient is…

- **steeper** than the dotted line, the object is travelling **faster** than the average speed
- **less steep** than the dotted line, the object is travelling **slower** than the average speed.

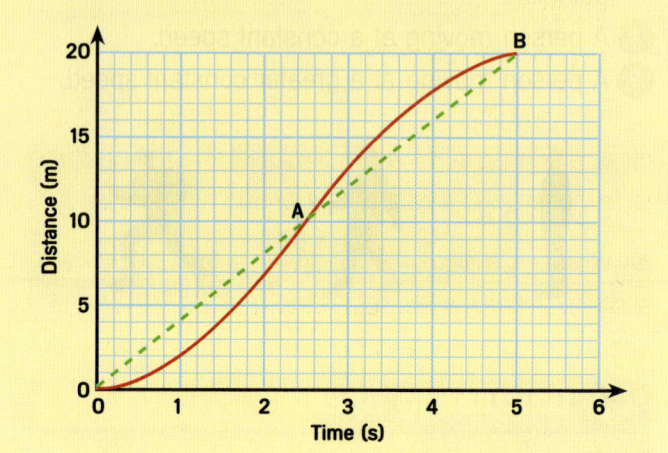

Velocity–Time Graphs

The slope, or **gradient**, of a **velocity–time graph** represents how quickly an object is increasing in speed (i.e. **accelerating**).

The steeper the slope, the faster its speed is increasing.

N.B. You need to be able to draw and interpret velocity–time graphs.

Velocity–time graphs are used in **lorry tachographs** to make sure that drivers…

- don't exceed the speed limit
- rest for suitable amounts of time.

Object is stationary.

Object is moving at a constant speed.

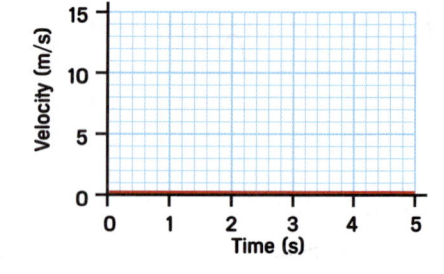

Object is accelerating.

Key Words

Acceleration • Force • Friction • Gradient • Gravity • Velocity–time graph

Explaining Motion

Forces

A **force** occurs when two objects **interact** with each other.

Whenever one object exerts a force on another it always experiences a force in return.

The forces in an **interaction pair** are…
- **equal** in size
- **opposite** in direction.

Gravity (**weight**) – two masses are attracted to each other, e.g. you are attracted to the Earth and the Earth is attracted to you with an equal and opposite force.

Air resistance (**drag**) – the air tries to slow down a skydiver by pushing upwards against him/her. The skydiver pushes the air out of the way with an equal and opposite force.

Rocket and jet engines – the engine pushes gas backwards (action) and the gas pushes the rocket forwards (reaction).

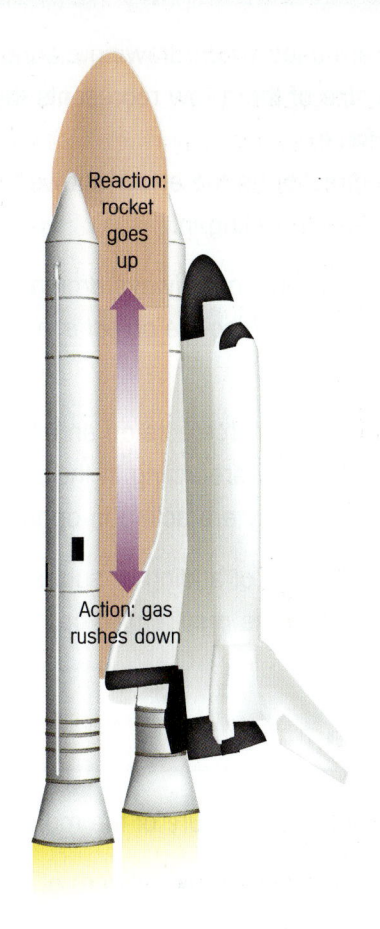

Reaction: rocket goes up

Action: gas rushes down

Friction and Reaction

Some forces only occur as a response to another force.

When an object is resting on a surface…
- the object is pulled down onto the surface by gravity
- the surface pushes up on the object with an equal force.

This is called the **reaction of the surface**.

When two objects try to slide past one another, both objects experience a force that tries to **stop them moving**.

This is called **friction**.

Objects don't have to be moving to experience friction. For example, the friction from a car's brakes stops it rolling down a hill.

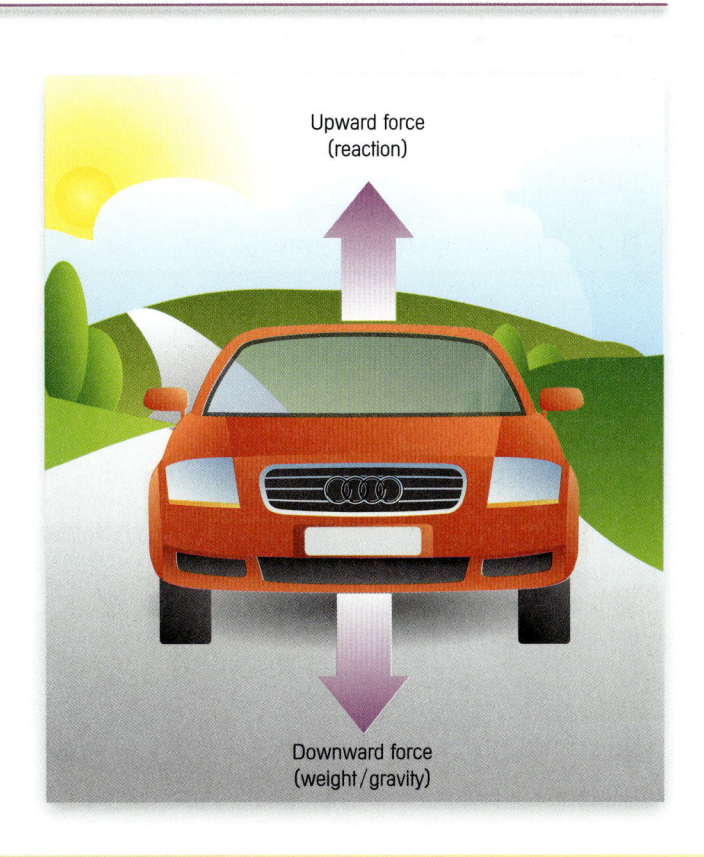

Upward force (reaction)

Downward force (weight/gravity)

43

Explaining Motion

Forces and Motion

Arrows are used when drawing diagrams of **forces**:
- The size of the arrow represents the size of the force.
- The direction of the arrow shows the direction the force is acting in.

N.B. Force arrows are always drawn with the tail of the arrow touching the object even if the force is pushing the object.

If more than one force acts on an object they will…
- add up if they are acting in the same direction
- subtract if they are acting in opposite directions.

The overall effect of adding or subtracting these forces is called the **resultant force**.

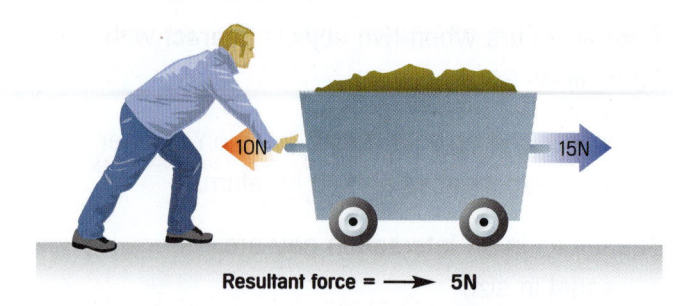

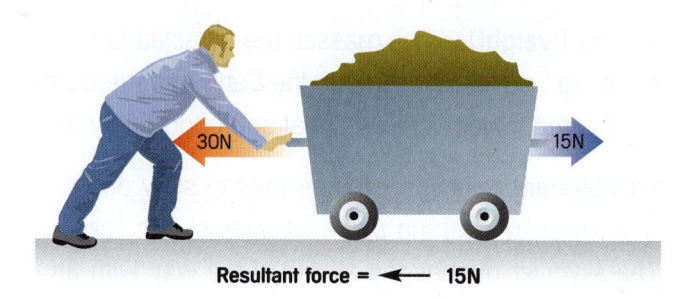

Resultant force = → 5N

Resultant force = ← 15N

Momentum

Momentum is a measure of the motion of an object.

You can calculate the momentum of an object using this formula:

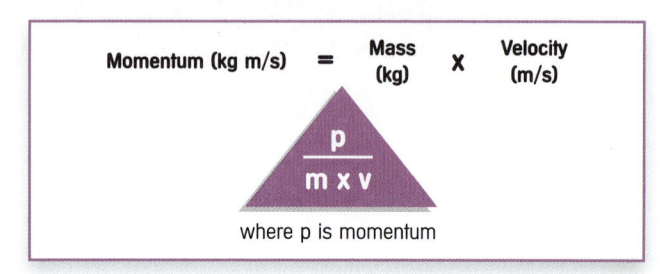

Momentum (kg m/s) = Mass (kg) × Velocity (m/s)

$$\frac{p}{m \times v}$$

where p is momentum

If a car and a lorry are travelling at the same speed, the lorry will have more momentum because it has a bigger mass.

Example

A car has a mass of 1200kg and is travelling at a velocity of 30m/s. What is its momentum?

Momentum = Mass × Velocity
= 1200kg × 30m/s
= **36 000kg m/s**

Explaining Motion

Change in Momentum

If the **resultant force** acting on an object is zero, its momentum will not change. So, if the object is…

- stationary, it will remain stationary
- already moving, it will continue moving in a straight line at a steady speed.

If the resultant force acting on an object is not zero, it causes a change of momentum in the direction of the force. This could…

- make a stationary object move
- increase or decrease an object's speed
- change an object's direction.

The extent of the change in momentum depends on…

- the size of the resultant force
- the length of time the force is acting on the object.

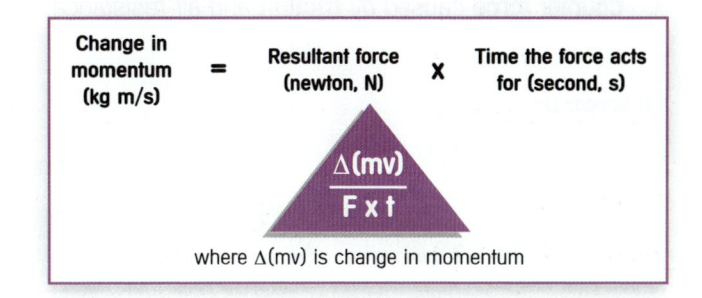

| Change in momentum (kg m/s) | = | Resultant force (newton, N) | × | Time the force acts for (second, s) |

$$\frac{\Delta(mv)}{F \times t}$$

where Δ(mv) is change in momentum

Collisions

Collisions cause changes in momentum.

For example, a car with a mass of 1000kg, travelling at 10m/s, has a momentum of 10 000kg m/s. If the car is involved in a collision and comes to a sudden stop, it would experience a change in momentum of 10 000kg m/s.

Sudden changes in momentum as a result of a collision can affect…

- the car
- the passengers – leading to injuries.

If the change in momentum is spread out over a longer period of time, the resultant force will be smaller.

Safety Devices

The force of the **impact** on the human body can be reduced by increasing the **time** of the impact.

This is the purpose of road safety devices, for example…

- seat-belts
- crumple zones – crumple on impact (e.g. motorcycle and bicycle helmets)
- air bags.

Crumple zone

Key Words
Force • Momentum • Resultant force

Explaining Motion

Speeding Up and Slowing Down

Cars and bicycles have a...
- **driving force** produced by the engine (car) or the energy of the cyclist (bicycle)
- **counter force** caused by **friction** and air resistance.

If the driving force is...
- **bigger than** the counter force, the vehicle speeds up
- **equal to** the counter force, the vehicle travels at a constant speed in a straight line
- **smaller than** the counter force, the vehicle slows down.

Car Speeds Up

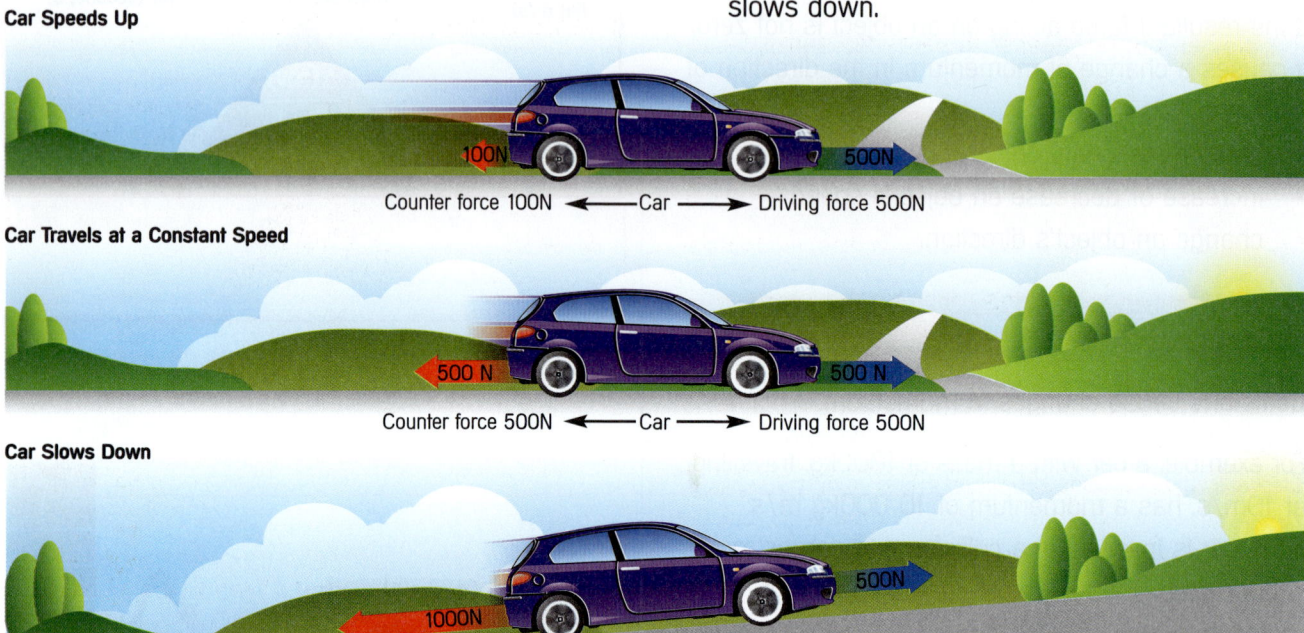

Counter force 100N ← Car → Driving force 500N

Car Travels at a Constant Speed

Counter force 500N ← Car → Driving force 500N

Car Slows Down

Counter force 1000N ← Car → Driving force 500N

Kinetic Energy

A moving object has **kinetic energy**.

The amount of kinetic energy an object has depends on its...
- **mass**
- **velocity**.

The greater the mass and velocity of an object, the more kinetic energy it has. You can calculate kinetic energy using this formula:

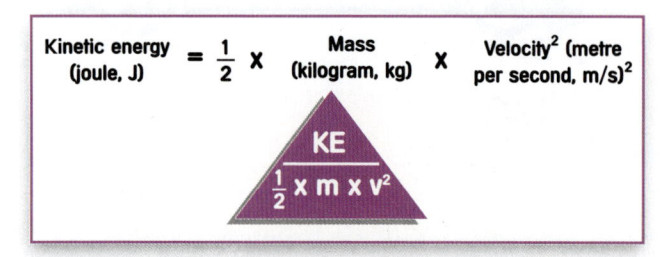

Kinetic energy (joule, J) = $\frac{1}{2}$ × Mass (kilogram, kg) × Velocity^2 (metre per second, m/s)^2

$$\frac{KE}{\frac{1}{2} \times m \times v^2}$$

Example

A bicycle of mass 50kg is moving at a velocity of 8m/s. How much kinetic energy does it have?

Kinetic energy = $\frac{1}{2}$ × Mass × Velocity^2
= $\frac{1}{2}$ × 50kg × (8m/s)^2
= $\frac{1}{2}$ × 50 × 64
= **1600J**

Explaining Motion

Work and Energy

Work is done by a force to move an object, resulting in the **transfer** of **energy**.

When work is done…
- **on** an object, the object **gains** energy
- **by** an object, the object **loses** energy.

The total amount of energy remains the same, i.e. energy is **conserved**.

Change in Energy (joule, J) = Work done (joule, J)

When a force makes an object's velocity increase…
- work is done on the object
- the object gains kinetic energy.

If you ignore drag and friction, the increase in kinetic energy will be **equal to** the work done by the force. But, in reality, some of the energy will be dissipated (lost) as heat.

The relationship between work done, force and distance is shown by the formula:

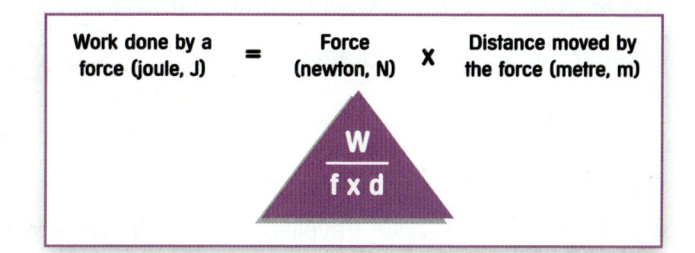

Work done by a force (joule, J) = Force (newton, N) x Distance moved by the force (metre, m)

$$\frac{W}{f \times d}$$

Gravitational Potential Energy

When an object is lifted above the ground…
- work is done by the lifting force against gravity
- the object has the potential to do work when it falls, e.g. a diver standing on a diving board.

This is called **gravitational potential energy** (**GPE**).

You can calculate change in GPE using this formula:

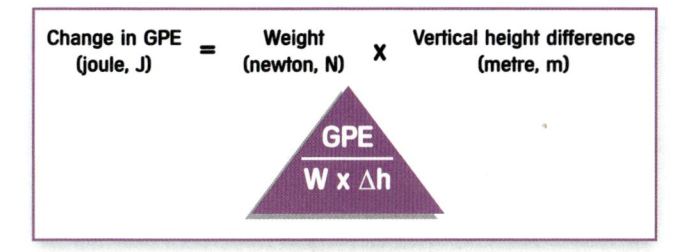

Change in GPE (joule, J) = Weight (newton, N) x Vertical height difference (metre, m)

$$\frac{GPE}{W \times \Delta h}$$

N.B. To find the GPE, you use weight not mass.

If an object is dropped, its GPE decreases and converts into kinetic energy.

Example
An object is dropped from a height of 5m. It has a mass of 2kg and weighs 20N. How much kinetic energy does it gain?

Change in GPE = Weight x Vertical height difference
= 20N x 5m
= **100J**

The object…
- loses 100J of gravitational potential energy
- gains 100J of kinetic energy.

HT You can use the kinetic energy formula to work out the velocity of a falling object. In the example above we know that the object has gained 100J of kinetic energy.

Kinetic energy = $\frac{1}{2}$ x Mass x Velocity^2

$100 = \frac{1}{2} \times 2 \times V^2$

$100 = V^2$

$V = \sqrt{100}$

= 10m/s

Key Words
Force • Friction • Kinetic energy • Velocity

Module P4 Summary

Speed

Speed = How fast an object is moving.

Instantaneous speed = Speed of an object at a particular point in time.

$$\text{Speed (m/s)} = \frac{\text{Distance travelled (m)}}{\text{Time taken (s)}}$$

Distance–Time Graphs

The **gradient** of a distance–time graph represents the **speed** of an object.

Steeper the slope ➡ **Greater** the speed.

HT To calculate speed using a distance–time graph:
1. Take any two points on the gradient.
2. Read off the distance travelled between these points.
3. Note the time taken between these points.
4. Divide the distance by the time.

Curvy distance–time graphs = Speed of an object is changing.

Average speed of a curvy distance–time graph = Total distance divided by total time.

Gradient steeper than dotted line ➡ Object travelling faster than average speed.

Gradient less steep than dotted line ➡ Object travelling slower than average speed.

Velocity

Velocity = Describes an object's speed and direction.

The **gradient** of a velocity–time graph represents how quickly an object is increasing in speed.

Steeper the slope ➡ **Faster** the speed is increasing.

Velocity–time graphs are used in **lorry tachographs** to make sure that drivers rest regularly and don't exceed speed limits.

Forces

Force – occurs when two objects interact with each other.

Forces in an interaction pair are…
- equal in size
- opposite in direction.

Gravity = Force of attraction between all masses.

Air resistance = Air tries to slow an object down.

Module P4 Summary

Reaction of the surface = An object is pulled down onto the surface by gravity and the surface pushes up onto the object with an equal force.

Friction = The force that tries to stop two objects moving as they slide past one another.

Resultant force = Overall effect of adding or subtracting forces.

Size of force arrow = Size of force.

Direction of force arrow = Direction force is acting in.

Force arrows are always drawn with the tail of the arrow touching the object.

Momentum

Momentum = Measure of the motion of an object.

$$\text{Momentum (kg m/s)} = \text{Mass (kg)} \times \text{Velocity (m/s)}$$

$$\text{Change in momentum (kg m/s)} = \text{Resultant force (newton, N)} \times \text{Time the force acts for (second, s)}$$

Collisions cause a change in momentum.

If a change in momentum is **spread out** over a longer period of time, the resultant force will be **smaller**.

Increasing **time** of impact ➡ Reduces **force** of impact.

Energy

Kinetic energy = The energy an object has because of its movement. It depends on the mass and velocity of an object.

$$\text{Kinetic energy (joule, J)} = \frac{1}{2} \times \text{Mass (kilogram, kg)} \times \text{Velocity}^2 \text{ (metre per second, m/s)}^2$$

Work is done by a force to move an object, resulting in the **transfer** of energy.

Work done **on** an object ➡ Object **gains** energy.

Work done **by** an object ➡ Object **loses** energy.

$$\text{Work done by a force (joule, J)} = \text{Force (newton, N)} \times \text{Distance moved by the force (metre, m)}$$

Change in energy = Work done.

Gravitational potential energy = Energy an object has because of its mass and height above the Earth.

Object is dropped ➡ GPE decreases ➡ Kinetic energy increases.

$$\text{Change in GPE (joule, J)} = \text{Weight (newton, N)} \times \text{Vertical height difference (metre, m)}$$

Module P4 Practice Questions

1 Name two things that velocity tells you about an object.

a) _speed_   b) _direction_

2 A bus travels 20 metres in 5 seconds. What is its average speed?

_4 m/s_

3 What is instantaneous speed?

speed at a certain time

4 a) The graph shows three different journeys. Match statements **A**, **B** and **C** with the labels **1–3** on the graph.

A   The person is moving at the fastest speed. [3]

B   The person is moving at the slowest speed. [2]

C   The person is stationary. [1]

HT b) Using the graph above, calculate the average speed of journey three.

_5 m/s_

5 Explain why velocity–time graphs are used in lorry tachographs.

[illegible]

6 What is friction?

Force between 2 moving objects

7 Use the words from the list below, to complete the following paragraph.

add up   **resultant force**   **momentum**   **subtract**   **velocity**

If two forces are acting on an object in the same direction they will _add_. If they are acting on an object in opposite directions they will _subtract_. The overall effect is called the _resultant_.

50

Module P4 Practice Questions

8 Calculate the momentum of a car that has a mass of 1500kg and is travelling at a velocity of 45m/s.

67500 kgm/s

9 a) Name three road safety devices.

i) *crumple*   ii) *seatbelts*   iii) _____

b) Explain how safety devices reduce the force of impact on the human body.

10 If the driving force of a car is bigger than the counter force, what will happen to the car? Tick the correct option.

A The car will stop. ☐   B The car will slow down. ☐

C The car will speed up. ☑   D The car will travel at a constant speed. ☐

11 A lorry of mass 1200kg is moving at a velocity of 12m/s. How much kinetic energy does it have?

86400 J

12 If work is done by a force to move an object, what happens to the total amount of energy?

13 A ball is dropped from a height of 8m. It has a mass of 2kg and weighs 18N.

a) Calculate how much kinetic energy the ball gains as it falls.

b) How much gravitational potential energy does the ball lose?

144 J

HT c) Calculate the velocity of the falling ball just before it hits the ground.

144 = 0.5 × m × v²
12

Electric Circuits

Static Electricity

When you rub two objects together they become **electrically charged** as **electrons** (which are negatively charged) are transferred from one object to the other:
- The object **receiving** the electrons becomes **negatively** charged.
- The object **giving up** electrons becomes **positively** charged.

The electrical charge is called **static electricity**.

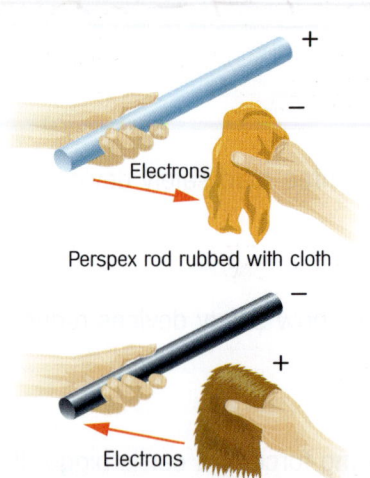

Perspex rod rubbed with cloth

Ebonite rod rubbed with fur

Repulsion and Attraction

When two charged materials are brought together, they exert a **force** on each other:
- Two materials with the same type of charge **repel** each other.
- Two materials with different charges **attract** each other.

For example, if you move…
- a positively charged Perspex rod near to another positively charged Perspex rod suspended on a string, the suspended rod will be **repelled**,
- a negatively charged ebonite rod near to a positively charged suspended Perspex rod, the suspended Perspex rod will be **attracted**.

N.B. You would get the same result with two ebonite rods.

N.B. You would get the same result if the rods were the other way round.

Electric Currents

An **electric current** is a **flow of charge**. It is measured in **amperes** (amps).

In an electric circuit…
- the components and wires are full of charges that are free to move
- the battery causes the free charges to move
- the charges are not used up but flow in a continuous loop.

In **metal conductors** there are lots of charges free to move, but in **insulators** there are no charges free to move. Metals contain **free electrons** in their structure, which move to create an **electric current**.

Key Words

Alternating current • Current • Direct current • Electron • Force • Potential difference • Static electricity • Voltage

Electric Circuits

Circuit Symbols

Standard symbols are used to represent components in circuits.

Cell		Fixed resistor	
Power supply (battery)		Variable resistor	
Filament lamp		Thermistor	
Switch (open) (closed)		Voltmeter	
Light dependent resistor (LDR)		Ammeter	

Types of Current

A **direct current** (d.c.) always flows in the same direction. Cells and batteries supply direct current.

An **alternating current** (a.c.) changes the direction of flow back and forth continuously and is used for mains electricity. The mains supply of **voltage** to your home is 230 volts.

HT Alternating current is used for mains supply instead of direct current. This is because…
- it's easier to generate
- it can be distributed more efficiently.

Potential Difference and Current

Potential difference is another name for **voltage**:
- It's a measure of the 'push' of the battery on the charges in the circuit.
- It's measured in **volts** (V) using a **voltmeter** connected in parallel across the component.

A bulb with 3 volts across it is taking 3 joules of energy from every unit of charge. This energy is given off as heat and light.

The greater the potential difference across a component, the greater the current will be.

When you add more batteries in series, the potential difference and the current increase.

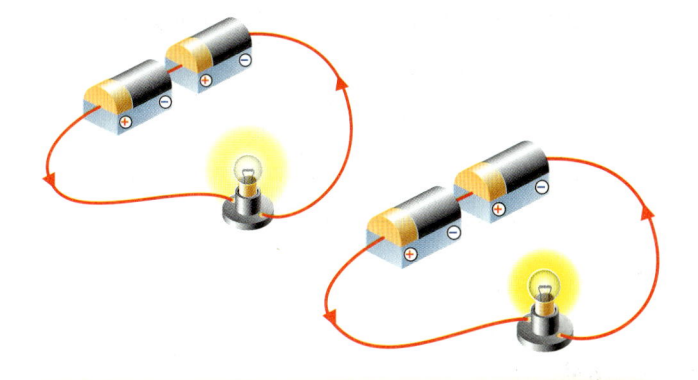

HT When you add more batteries in parallel…
- the total potential difference and current remain the same
- each battery supplies less current.

Electric Circuits

Resistance and Current

Components **resist** the flow of **charge** through them. Examples of components are…
- resistors
- lamps
- motors.

The connecting wires in the circuit have some **resistance** but it's so small that it's usually ignored.

The **greater the resistance** in a circuit, the **smaller the current** will be.

Two lamps together in a circuit with one cell have a certain resistance. If you include another cell in the circuit it provides…
- a greater **potential difference**
- a larger **current**.

When you add resistors in **series** the battery has to push charges through more resistors so the **resistance increases**.

When you add resistors in **parallel** there are more paths for the charges to flow along so the total **resistance reduces** and the total **current increases**.

When an electric current flows through a component it causes the component to heat up. This heating effect is large enough to make a lamp filament glow.

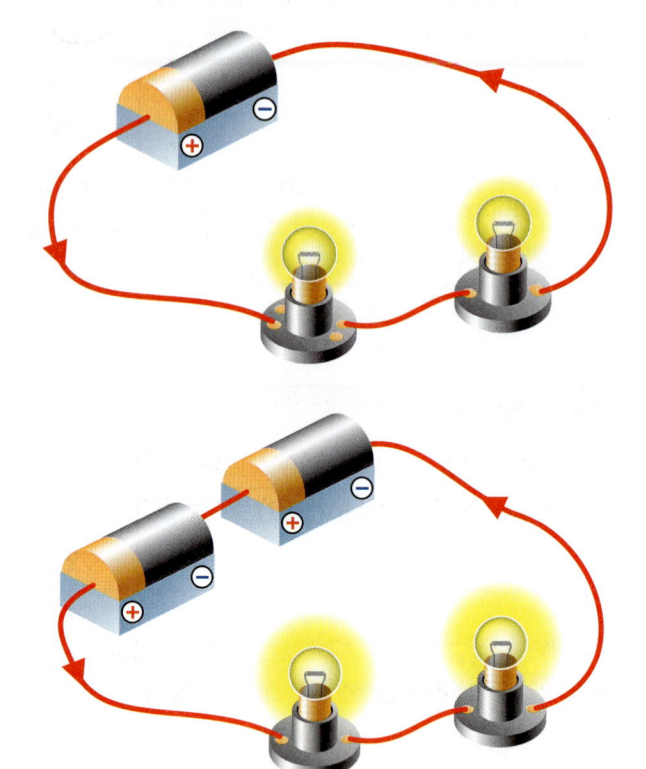

HT As the current flows…
- moving charges collide with the stationary atoms in the wire giving them energy
- the increase in energy causes the component to heat up.

Calculating Resistance

You can calculate resistance using this formula:

Resistance (ohm, Ω) = Potential difference (volt, V) / Current (ampere, A)

$$\frac{V}{I \times R}$$

where I is current

HT You can work out the voltage or current by rearranging the resistance formula.

Example
A circuit has a current of 0.2 amps and a bulb with a resistance of 15 ohms. What is the reading on the voltmeter?

Potential difference = Current x Resistance
= 0.2A x 15Ω
= **3V**

Example
A circuit has a current of 3 amps and a potential difference of 6V. What is the resistance?

Resistance = Potential difference / Current = 6V / 3A = **2Ω**

Electric Circuits

Current–Potential Difference Graphs

As long as a component's resistance stays constant, the current through the resistor is **directly proportional** to the **voltage** across the resistor. This is regardless of which direction the current is flowing.

This means that a graph showing current through the component, and voltage across the component, will be a **straight line** through 0.

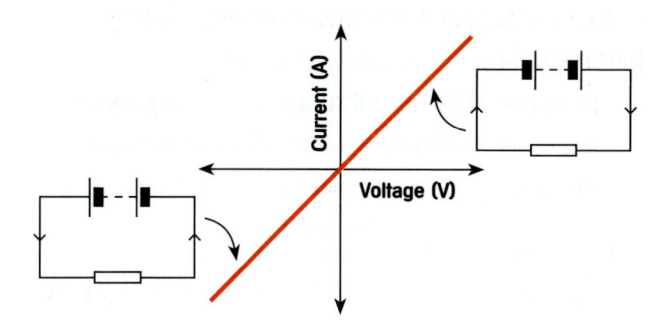

Thermistors and LDRs

The resistance of a **thermistor** depends on its temperature. As the temperature increases…
- its resistance decreases
- more current flows.

The resistance of a **light dependent resistor (LDR)** depends on light intensity. As the amount of light falling on it increases…
- its resistance decreases
- more current flows.

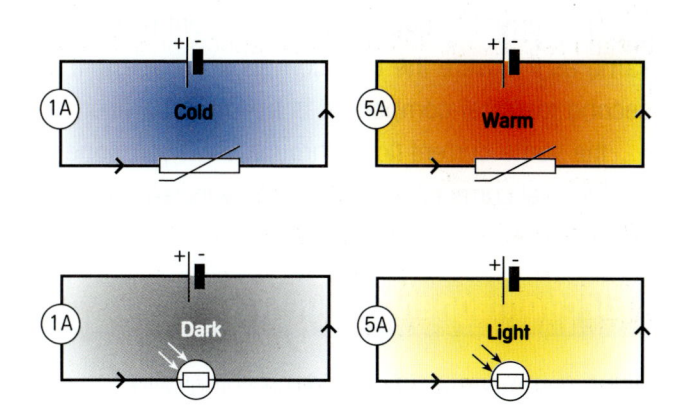

Series Circuits

In series circuits…
- the current flowing through each component is the same, i.e. $A_1 = A_2 = A_3$
- the potential difference across the components adds up to the potential difference across the battery, i.e. $V_1 = V_2 + V_3$
- the potential difference is largest across components with the greatest resistance.

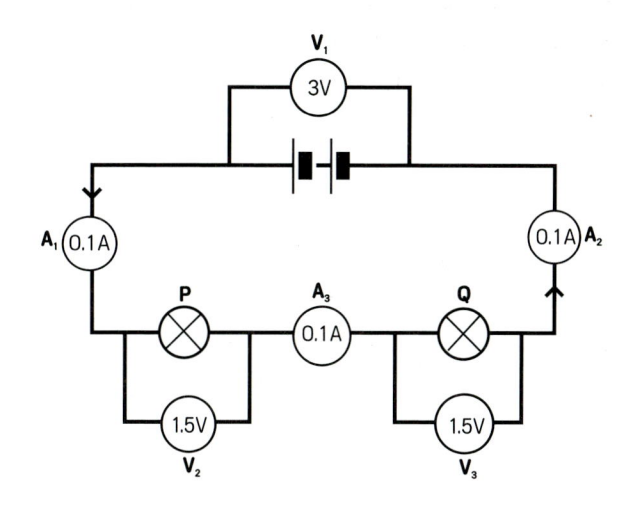

HT The total energy, transferred to each unit charge by the battery, must equal the total amount of energy transferred from the charge by the component.

More energy is transferred from the charge flowing through a greater resistance because it takes more energy to push the current through the resistor.

Key Words

Current • Potential difference • Resistance • Voltage

Electric Circuits

Parallel Circuits

In parallel circuits with one component per parallel path…
- the **current** flowing through each component depends on the **resistance** of each component
- the total current running from (and back to) the battery is equal to the sum of the current through each of the parallel components, i.e. $A_1 = A_2 + A_3 = A_4$
- the current is smallest through the component with the greatest resistance.

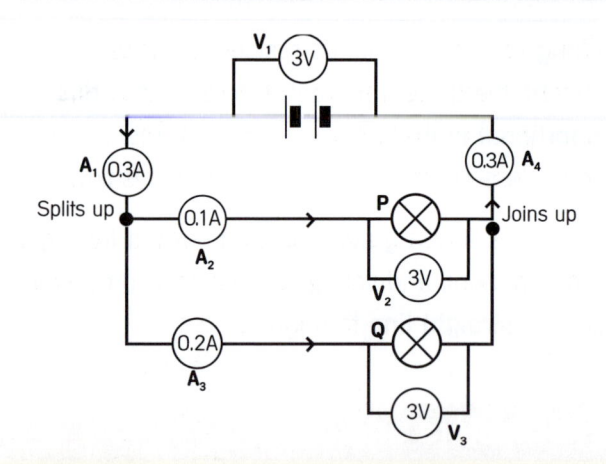

HT The current through each component is the same as if it were the only component present. If a second identical component is added in parallel…
- the same current flows through each component
- the total current through the battery increases.

The same **voltage** causes more current to flow through a smaller resistance than a bigger one.

The **potential difference** across each component is equal to the potential difference of the battery.

Electromagnetic Induction

When you move a magnet into a coil of wire, a **voltage** is induced between the ends of the wire because the magnetic field is being cut.

If the ends of the coil are connected to make a complete circuit, a **current** will be induced.

This is called **electromagnetic induction**.

Moving the magnet into the coil induces a current in one direction. You can then induce a current in the opposite direction by…
- moving the magnet out of the coil
- moving the other pole of the magnet into the coil.

If there's no movement of the coil or magnet, there's no induced current.

Moving the Magnet into the Coil

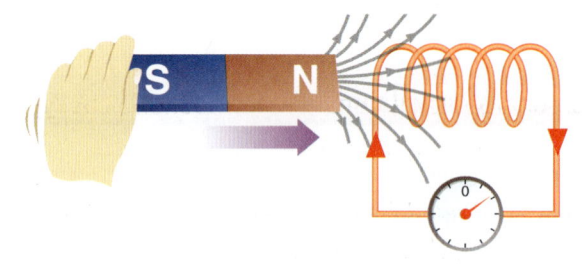

Moving the Magnet out of the Coil

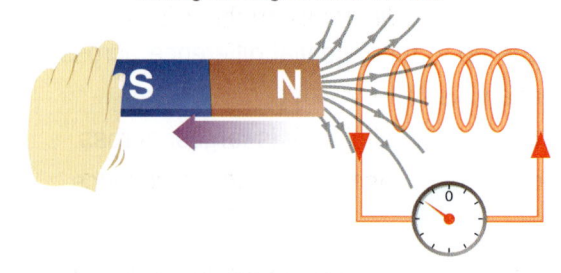

Moving the Other Pole of the Magnet into the Coil

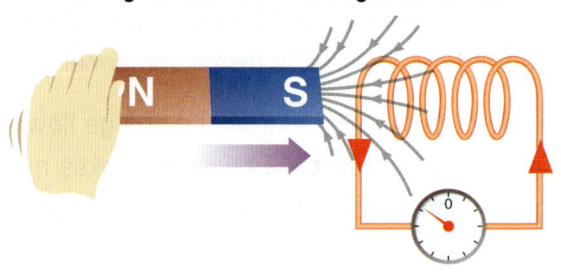

Key Words
Current • Resistance • Voltage

Electric Circuits

The Electric Generator

Mains electricity is produced by **generators**. Generators use the principle of **electromagnetic induction** to generate electricity by rotating a magnet inside a coil.

The size of the induced voltage can be increased by…
- increasing the speed of rotation of the magnet
- increasing the strength of the magnetic field
- increasing the number of turns on the coil
- placing an iron core inside the coil.

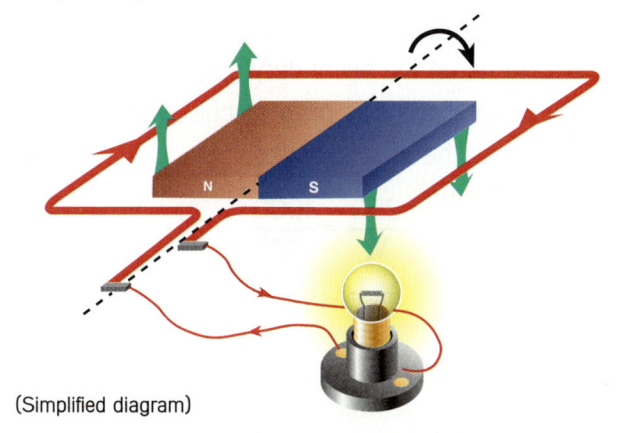

(Simplified diagram)

HT As the magnet rotates, the **voltage** induced in the coil changes direction and size as shown in the diagram.

The **current** that's produced is an **alternating current** as it reverses its direction of flow every half turn of the magnet.

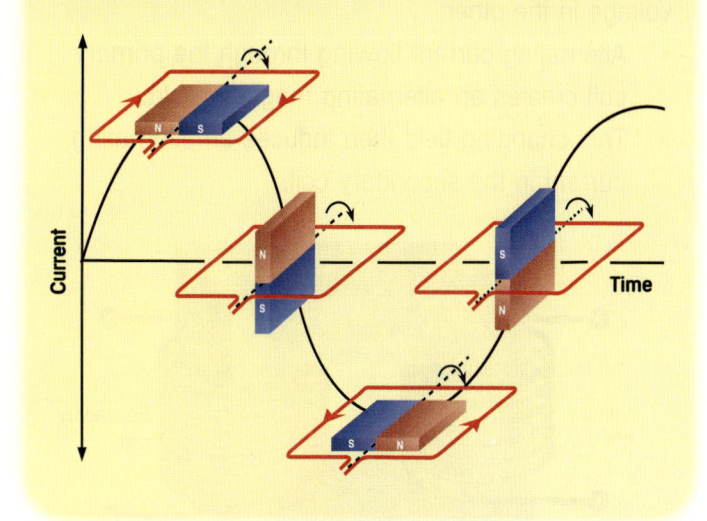

Power

When charge flows through a component, **energy is transferred** to the component.

Power is a measure of the rate of energy transfer and is measured in watts (W).

You can calculate power using the following formula:

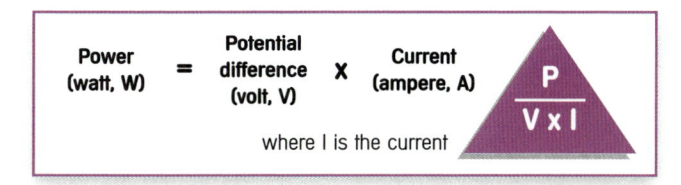

Power (watt, W) = Potential difference (volt, V) × Current (ampere, A)

$$\frac{P}{V \times I}$$

where I is the current

Example
An electric motor works at a current of 3A and a potential difference of 24V. What is the power of the motor?

Power = Potential Difference × Current
= 24V × 3A
= **72W**

HT You can work out the potential difference or current by rearranging the power formula.

Example
A 4W light bulb works at a current of 2A. What is the potential difference?

Potential difference = $\frac{\text{Power}}{\text{Current}} = \frac{4W}{2A} =$ **2V**

Electric Circuits

Transformers

Transformers are used to change the **voltage** of an **alternating current**. They consist of two coils of wire, called the primary and secondary coils, wrapped around a soft iron core.

When two coils of wire are close to each other, a changing magnetic field in one coil can induce a voltage in the other:
- Alternating current flowing through the primary coil creates an alternating magnetic field.
- This changing field then induces an alternating current in the secondary coil.

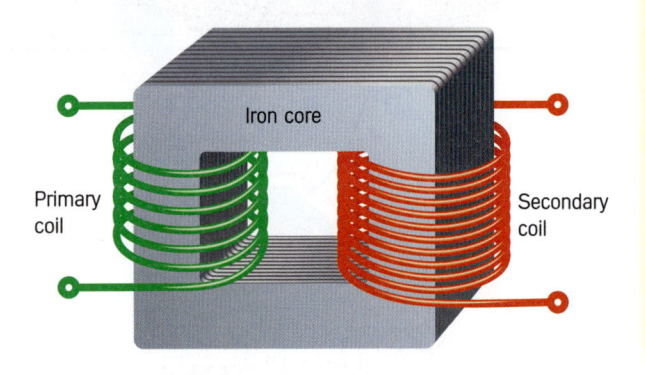

HT The amount by which a transformer changes the voltage depends on the number of turns on the primary and secondary coils. You need to be able to use this equation:

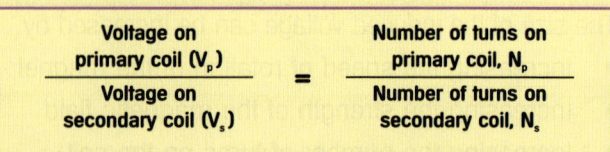

$$\frac{\text{Voltage on primary coil } (V_p)}{\text{Voltage on secondary coil } (V_s)} = \frac{\text{Number of turns on primary coil, } N_p}{\text{Number of turns on secondary coil, } N_s}$$

Example
A transformer has 1000 turns on the primary coil and 200 turns on the secondary coil. If a voltage of 250V is applied to the primary coil, what is the voltage across the secondary coil?

$$\frac{250}{V_s} = \frac{1000}{200}$$

$$250 = 5V_s$$

$$V_s = \frac{250}{5}$$

$$V_s = \mathbf{50V}$$

Energy

Energy is measured is **joules**. A joule is a very small amount of energy so a domestic electricity meter measures the energy transfer in **kilowatt hours**.

You can calculate energy transfer in joules and kilowatt hours using the following formula:

Energy transferred (joule, J) (kilowatt hour, kWh)	=	Power (watt, W) (Kilowatt, kW)	x	Time (second, s) (hour, h)

Example 1
A 30W light bulb is switched on for 45 seconds. What is the energy transferred in joules?

Energy transferred = Power x Time
= 30W x 45s
= **1350J**

Example 2
A 2000W electric hot plate is switched on for 90 minutes. What is the energy transferred in kWh?

Energy transferred = 2kW x 1.5h
= **3kWh**

HT You can work out the power or time by rearranging the energy transfer formula.

Example
A hairdryer is switched on for 6 minutes and the total energy transferred is 0.2kWh. What is the power rating of the hairdryer?

Power = $\frac{\text{Energy transferred}}{\text{Time}}$ = $\frac{0.2\text{kWh}}{0.1\text{h}}$ = **2kW**

Electric Circuits

Cost of Electricity

If you know the power, time and cost per kilowatt hour, you can calculate the cost of the electrical energy used. The formula is as follows:

Total cost = Number of units (kWh) x Cost per unit

Example

A 2000W electric fire is switched on for 30 minutes. How much does it cost if electricity is 8p per unit (kWh)?

Energy transferred = 2kW x 0.5h
= 1kWh (or 1 unit)
Cost = 1kWh x 8p
= **8p**

Efficiency of Appliances

The greater the proportion of energy that is usefully transferred, the more **efficient** the appliance is.

You can calculate efficiency using this formula:

$$\text{Efficiency (\%)} = \frac{\text{Energy usefully transferred}}{\text{Total energy supplied}} \times 100$$

Electrical Appliance	Energy In	Useful Energy Out	Efficiency
Light bulb	100 joules/s	Light: 20 joules/s	$\frac{20}{100} \times 100\%$ = **20%**
Kettle	2000 joules/s	Heat (in water): 1800 joules/s	$\frac{1800}{2000} \times 100\%$ = **90%**
Electric motor	500 joules/s	Kinetic: 300 joules/s	$\frac{300}{500} \times 100\%$ = **60%**
Television	200 joules/s	Light: 20 joules/s Sound: 30 joules/s	$\frac{50}{200} \times 100\%$ = **25%**

Key Words

Alternating current • Efficiency • Transformer • Voltage

Module P5 Summary

Static Electricity

Static electricity is created when two objects are rubbed together.

Objects receiving electrons ➡ Negatively charged.

Objects giving up electrons ➡ Positively charged.

Two materials with **same** charges ➡ **Repel** each other.

Two materials with **different** charges ➡ **Attract** each other.

Current and Potential Difference

Current = Flow of charge measured in amperes.

Direct current ➡ Flows in same direction.

Alternating current ➡ Constantly changes direction.

Metal conductors ➡ Lots of charges free to move.

Insulators ➡ No charges free to move.

Potential difference = Voltage ➡ Measured in volts.

Greater **potential difference** across a component ➡ Greater **current** through the component.

Adding batteries in series ➡ Increases voltage and current.

HT Adding batteries in parallel ➡ Potential difference and current stays same and each battery supplies less current.

Resistance

Components – resist flow of charge.

Electric current flows through component ➡ Component heats up.

Greater **resistance** in a circuit ➡ **Smaller** current.

Adding resistors in series ➡ Increases total resistance.

Adding resistors in parallel ➡ Reduces total resistance and increases current through the battery.

Current–potential difference graphs – current through resistor is directly proportional to voltage across resistor.

Thermistor – resistance depends on temperature.

LDR – resistance depends on light intensity.

$$\text{Resistance (ohm, }\Omega\text{)} = \frac{\text{Potential difference (volt, V)}}{\text{Current (ampere, A)}}$$

Module P5 Summary

Circuits

In **series circuits**…
- current flowing through each component is the same
- potential difference across components add up to that across the battery
- potential difference is **largest** across components with **greatest** resistance.

In **parallel circuits**…
- current flowing through each component depends on resistance
- current running to and from battery is equal to sum of current through each parallel component
- current is **smallest** across components with **greatest** resistance.

Circuit symbols are used to represent components in circuits.

Electromagnetic Induction

When a magnet is moved into a coil of wire, a **voltage** is induced. If ends of coil are connected, a **current** is induced.

Current can be induced in opposite direction by…
- moving magnet out of coil
- moving other pole of magnet into coil.

Electric generators – use electromagnetic induction. Produce mains electricity.

(HT) Generators produce alternating current as the direction of flow is reversed every half turn of the magnet.

Transformers – used to change the voltage of an alternating current.

Power and Energy

Power = measure of the rate of energy transfer.

Power (watt, W) = Potential difference (volt, V) × Current (ampere, A)

where I is the current

$$P = V \times I$$

Energy – measured in joules. Domestic energy is measured in kilowatt hours as joules are very small amounts of energy.

Energy transferred (joule, J) (kilowatt hour, kWh) = Power (watt, W) (Kilowatt, kW) × Time (second, s) (hour, h)

Efficiency = the proportion of energy that is usefully transferred by an appliance.

$$\text{Efficiency (\%)} = \frac{\text{Energy usefully transferred}}{\text{Total energy supplied}} \times 100$$

Module P5 Practice Questions

1 Peter has suspended a positively charged Perspex rod on a string.

   a) What will happen if Peter moves another positively charged Perspex rod near to it? _repel_

   b) What will happen if he moves a negatively charged ebonite rod near to it? _attract_

2 Draw the symbol for a cell.

[cell symbol drawn: —|‌|—]

3 This question is about currents.

   a) Fill in the missing words to complete the sentences below.

   _dc_ currents always flow in the same direction.

   _ac_ currents change the direction of flow back and forth continuously.

   HT b) Give two reasons why an alternating current is used for mains electricity.

   i) _easier to distribute_   ii) _generate_

4 a) What is another name for potential difference? _voltage_

   b) (Circle) the correct option in the following sentence:

   The greater the potential difference, the **lower** / **greater** the current will be. _[greater circled]_

5 a) A circuit has a current of 5 amps and a potential difference of 15 volts. Calculate the resistance.

   _3_

   HT b) A circuit has a current of 0.6 amps and a lamp with a resistance of 20 ohms. Calculate the potential difference.

   _12_

   c) Explain why, in series circuits, the potential difference is largest across components with the greatest resistance.

Module P5 Practice Questions

6 Sunita is experimenting with a magnet and a coil of wire. She moves the magnet into the coil to induce a current in one direction. Give two ways in which she can then induce a current in the opposite direction.

a) *change pole*   b) *take it out*

7 a) What are transformers used for?

change voltage

b) Briefly explain how transformers work.

Two coils of wire, soft iron core

HT c) A transformer has 2000 turns on the primary coil and 100 turns on the secondary coil. If a voltage of 400V is applied to the primary coil, what is the voltage across the secondary coil?

20

8 This question is about energy.

a) What unit is energy measured in? *J*

b) Why does a domestic electricity meter measure energy transfer in kilowatt hours?

larger

c) A 40W light bulb is switched on for 30 seconds. Calculate the amount of energy transferred in joules.

1200 J

d) A 1800W hairdryer is switched on for 30 minutes. Calculate the energy transferred in kilowatt hours.

900

9 Complete the table about the efficiency of the electrical appliances.

Electrical Appliance	Energy In	Useful Energy Out	Efficiency
Iron	2000 joules/s	Heat: 1600 joules/s	a)
Radio	200 joules/s	Sound: 60 joules/s	b)
Computer	400 joules/s	Light: 180 joules/s Sound: 80 joules/s	c)

The Wave Model of Radiation

Types of Waves

Waves are regular patterns of disturbance that transfer energy from one point to another without transferring particles of matter.

There are two types of wave:
- **Longitudinal**.
- **Transverse**.

In **longitudinal waves**, each particle…
- vibrates to and fro about its normal position
- moves backwards and forwards in the same plane as the direction of wave movement.

Sound travels as longitudinal waves.

In **transverse waves**, each particle…
- vibrates up and down about its normal position
- moves up and down at right angles (90°) to the direction of wave movement.

Light and **water** ripples both travel as transverse waves.

In these diagrams, the movement of coils in a slinky spring is used to represent the movement of particles in waves.

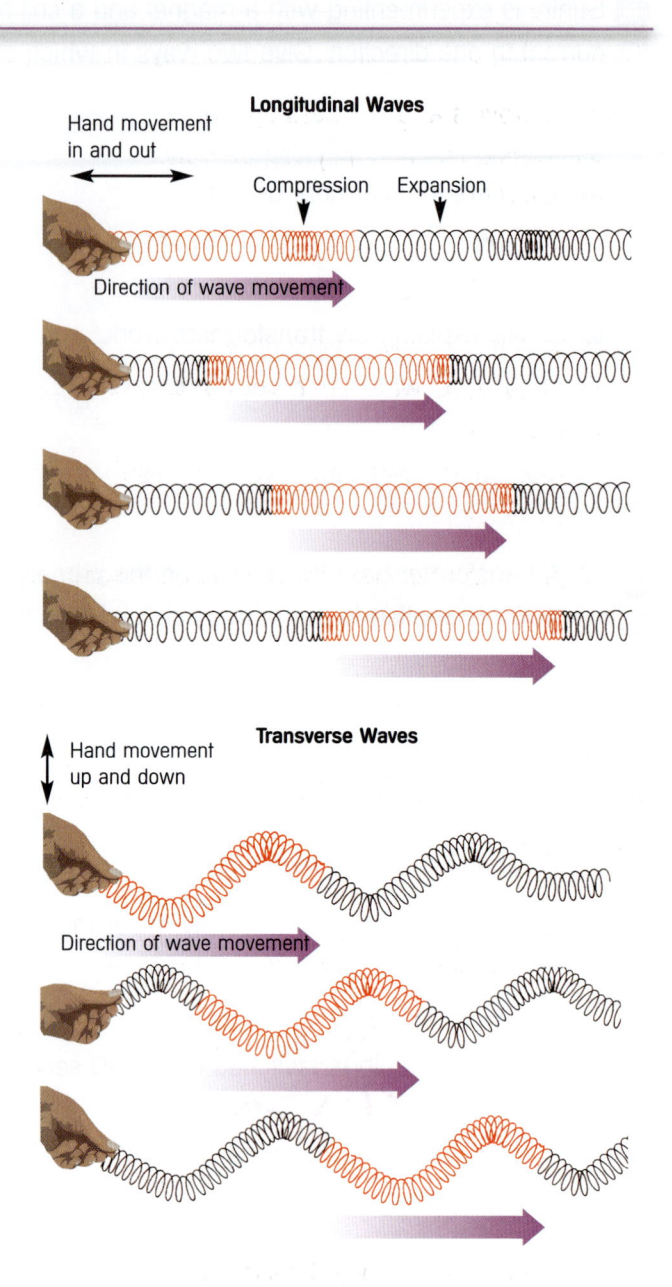

Wave Features

All waves have several important features:
- **Amplitude** – the maximum disturbance caused by a wave, measured by the distance from a crest (or trough) of the wave to the undisturbed position.
- **Wavelength** – the distance between corresponding points on two adjacent disturbances.
- **Frequency** – the number of waves produced, (or passing a particular point) in one second. Frequency is measured in **hertz** (Hz).

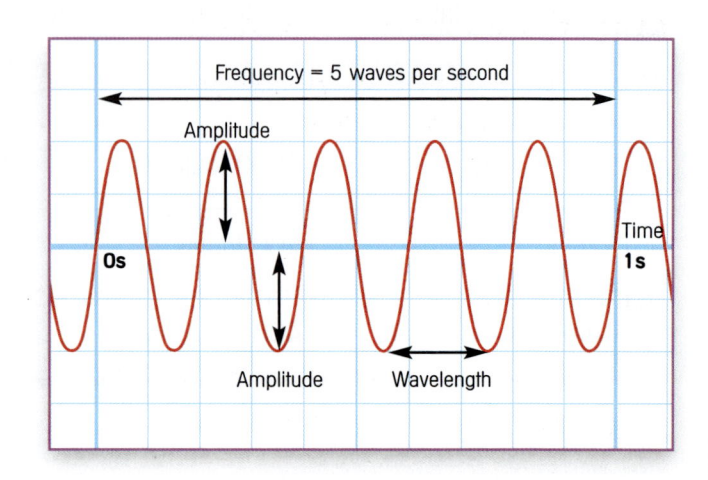

The Wave Model of Radiation

Wave Speed and Frequency

If a wave travels at a constant speed…
- **increasing** its frequency will **decrease** its wavelength
- **decreasing** its frequency will **increase** its wavelength.

If a wave has a constant frequency…
- **decreasing** its wave speed will **decrease** its wavelength
- **increasing** its wave speed will **increase** its wavelength.

N.B. *The speed of a wave is usually independent of its frequency and amplitude.*

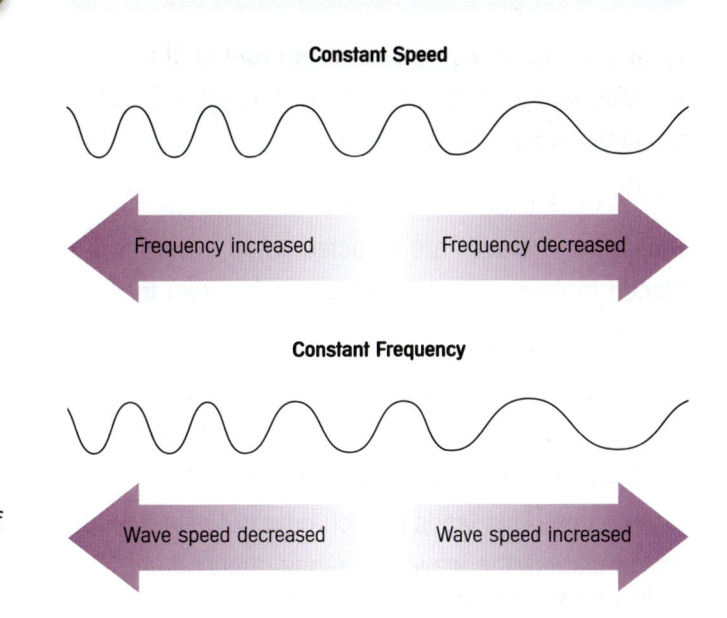

Constant Speed

Frequency increased ← → Frequency decreased

Constant Frequency

Wave speed decreased ← → Wave speed increased

The Wave Equation

Wave speed, frequency and wavelength are related by this formula:

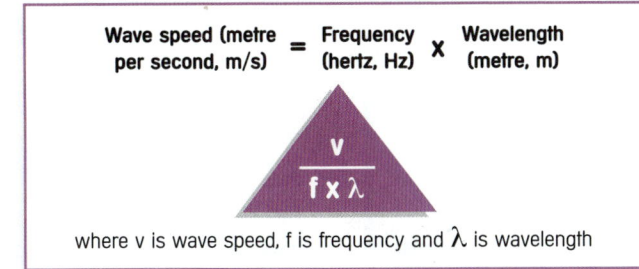

Wave speed (metre per second, m/s) = Frequency (hertz, Hz) × Wavelength (metre, m)

$$v = f \times \lambda$$

where v is wave speed, f is frequency and λ is wavelength

Example
A tuning fork of frequency 480Hz produces sound waves with a wavelength of 70cm when it is tapped. What is the speed of the wave?

Wave speed = Frequency × Wavelength
= 480Hz × 0.7m
= **336m/s**

HT You can work out the frequency or wavelength by rearranging the wave speed formula.

Example
Radio 5 Live transmits on a frequency of 909 000Hz. If the speed of radio waves is 300 000 000m/s, on what wavelength does it transmit?

Wavelength = $\dfrac{\text{Wave speed}}{\text{Frequency}}$

= $\dfrac{300\ 000\ 000\text{m/s}}{909\ 000\text{Hz}}$

= **330m**

Key Words
Amplitude • Frequency • Longitudinal • Transverse • Wavelength

The Wave Model of Radiation

Behaviour of Waves

Light, water and sound waves can be…
- *reflected*
- *refracted*
- *diffracted*.

Reflection – waves are reflected when a barrier is placed in their path. This effect can be seen in water waves.

Refraction – when waves cross a boundary between one medium and another, the *frequency* remains the same but there is a change in *wavelength*. This leads to a change in wave speed, which causes the wave to change direction.

Diffraction – when waves move through a narrow gap or past an obstacle they spread out from the edges. This is called diffraction. Diffraction is most obvious when…
- the size of the gap is similar to, or smaller than, the wavelength of the wave
- the waves which pass obstacles have long wavelengths.

Light waves need a very small gap to be diffracted.

The fact that light and sound can be diffracted provides evidence of their wave nature.

Reflection

Incident wave → *Barrier* → *Reflected wave*

Refraction

Shallow water / Boundary / Deep water
Refracted wave / Incident wave
Change in direction due to change in wave speed

Diffraction

Slight diffraction → Increased diffraction

Diffraction

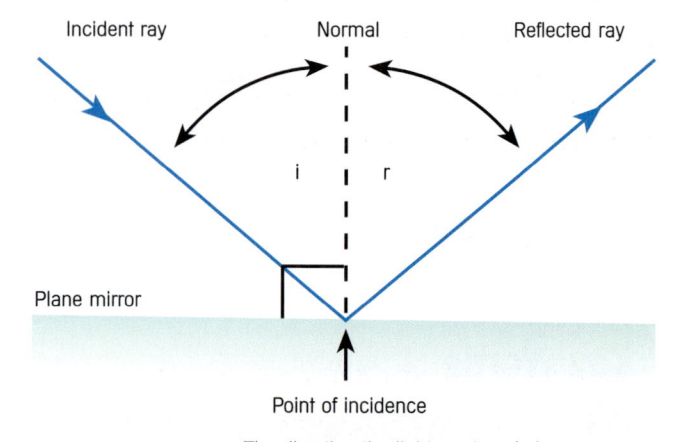

Slight diffraction → Increased diffraction

Reflection of Light

Light is **reflected** when it strikes a surface. This diagram shows light reflected in a plane mirror:
- The **normal line** is perpendicular to the reflecting surface at the point of incidence. It's used to calculate the angles of incidence and reflection.
- The **incident ray** is the light ray travelling **towards** the mirror.
- The **reflected ray** is the light ray travelling **away** from the mirror.

Angle of incidence = Angle of reflection

Incident ray — Normal — Reflected ray
i / r
Plane mirror
Point of incidence

→ = The direction the light ray travels in
i = Angle of incidence
r = Angle of reflection

The Wave Model of Radiation

Refraction of Light at an Interface

Light…
- changes direction when it crosses a boundary between one medium and another
- continues straight on when it meets the boundary at an angle of 90° (i.e. along the normal).

When the angle of refraction is **greater than 90°** the light can't escape from the medium and is reflected.

This is called **total internal reflection**.

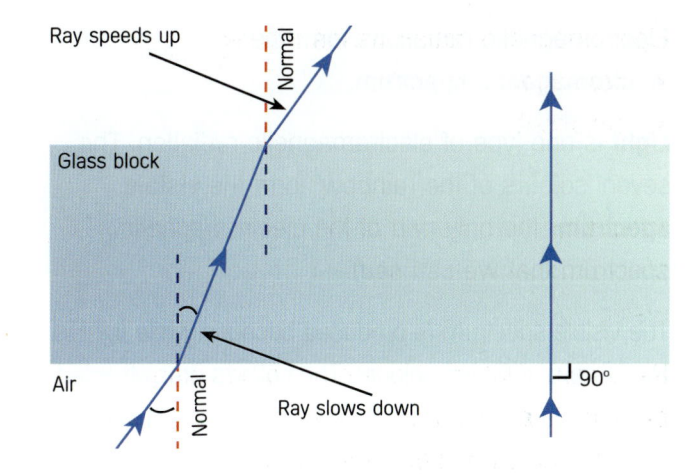

Interference

When two waves meet, their effects can add up. This is called **interference**.

Constructive interference is when…
- two waves arrive in step – the peak of one wave coincides with the peak of another
- the waves reinforce each other and their amplitudes add up.

Destructive interference is when…
- two waves arrive out of step – the peak of one wave meets the trough of another
- the waves cancel each other out.

Two rays of light can be shown to produce an **interference pattern**. If the light from one ray arriving at the screen is either **in step** or **out of step** with the other ray, it produces this pattern.

The interference of light and sound provides further evidence of their wave nature.

Key Words

Amplitude • Diffraction • Frequency • Interference • Reflection • Refraction • Wavelength

67

The Wave Model of Radiation

Electromagnetic Radiation

Electromagnetic radiations form the **electromagnetic spectrum**.

Light is one type of electromagnetic radiation. The seven 'colours of the rainbow' form the **visible spectrum** (the only part of the electromagnetic spectrum that we can see).

The visible spectrum is produced because white light is made up of different colours. The colours are **refracted** by different amounts as they pass through a prism:
- Red light is refracted the least.
- Violet light is refracted the most.

This is because the different colours have...
- different **frequencies**
- different **wavelengths**.

The intensity of a beam of radiation depends on the number of **photons** (packets of energy) it delivers every second.

HT The intensity of the beam also depends on the **amount of energy** carried by each **photon**.

All electromagnetic waves travel through space (a vacuum) at the same, very high, speed.

Electromagnetic waves are very different from sound waves:
- Electromagnetic waves can travel through empty space.
- Sound waves need a medium (solid, liquid or gas) to travel through.

Key Words

Electromagnetic spectrum • Frequency • Photon • Reflection • Refraction • Wavelength

The Electromagnetic Spectrum

- Glass prism
- White light
- Low frequency, Low photon energy
- Radio waves
- Microwaves
- Infrared rays
- Visible light
- Ultraviolet rays
- X-rays
- Gamma rays
- High frequency, High photon energy

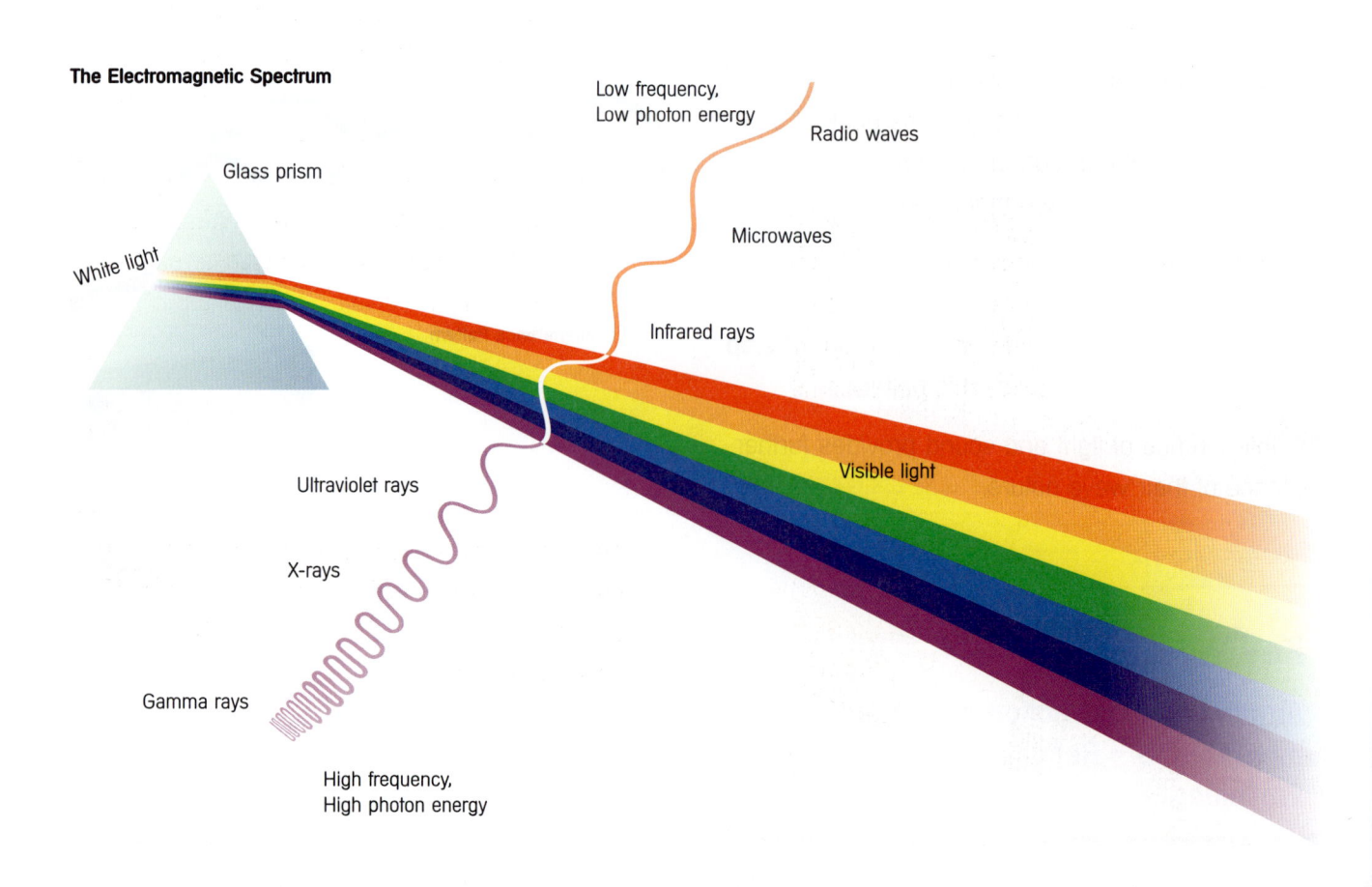

The Wave Model of Radiation

Uses of Electromagnetic Waves

Different electromagnetic waves have **different frequencies**.

They can be used for different purposes depending on how much they are **reflected**, **absorbed** or **transmitted** by different materials.

Their signals can be carried by…
- radio waves and microwaves (through the Earth's atmosphere and space)
- light waves and infrared waves (through optical fibres).

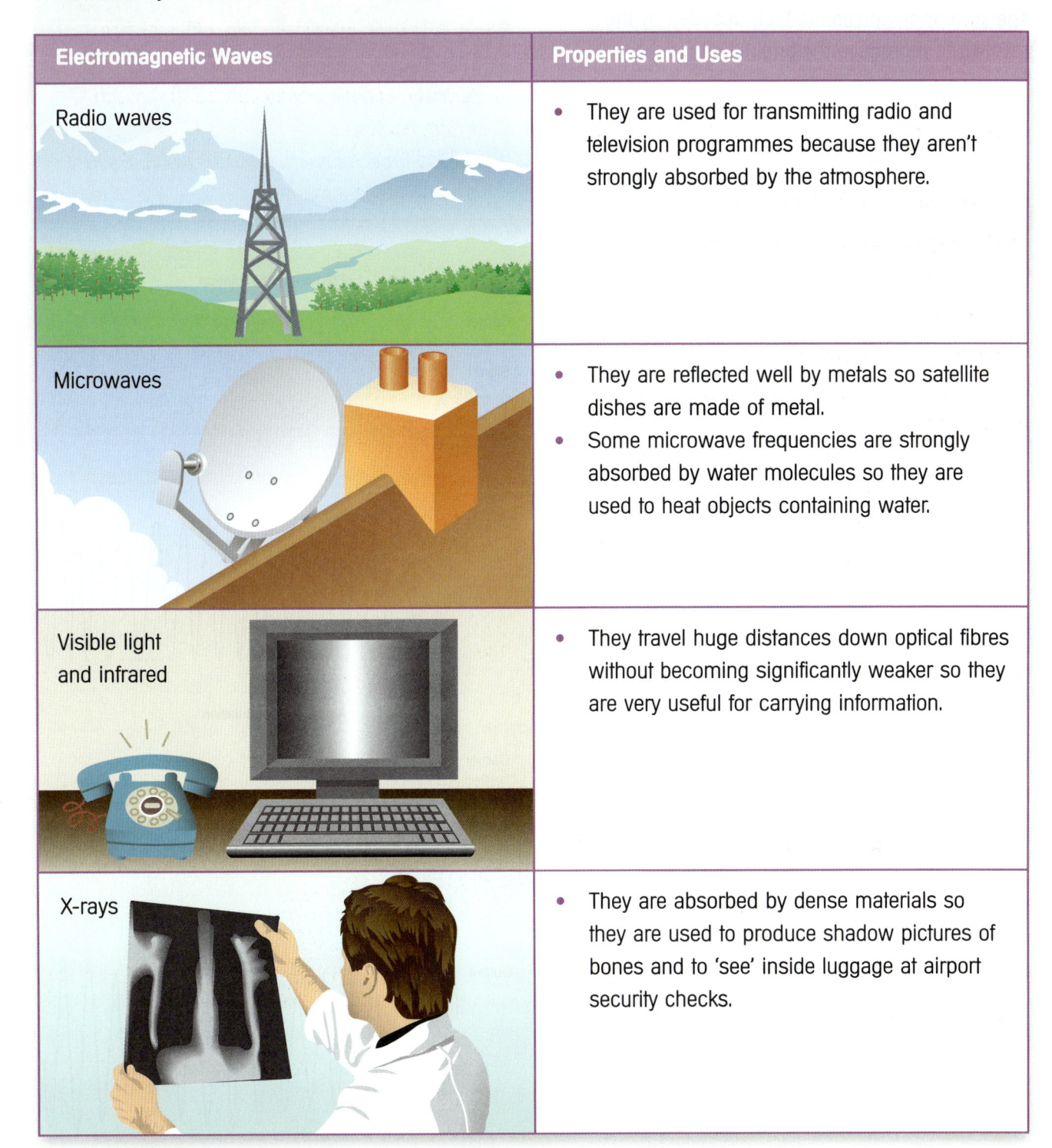

Electromagnetic Waves	Properties and Uses
Radio waves	• They are used for transmitting radio and television programmes because they aren't strongly absorbed by the atmosphere.
Microwaves	• They are reflected well by metals so satellite dishes are made of metal. • Some microwave frequencies are strongly absorbed by water molecules so they are used to heat objects containing water.
Visible light and infrared	• They travel huge distances down optical fibres without becoming significantly weaker so they are very useful for carrying information.
X-rays	• They are absorbed by dense materials so they are used to produce shadow pictures of bones and to 'see' inside luggage at airport security checks.

69

The Wave Model of Radiation

Modulation

For a wave to carry a signal it must be **modulated**. This process involves making the wave vary either in **amplitude** or **frequency** to create a variation in the original wave. It's this pattern of variation that carries the information.

The pattern of variation is then decoded by the receiver to reproduce the original sound.

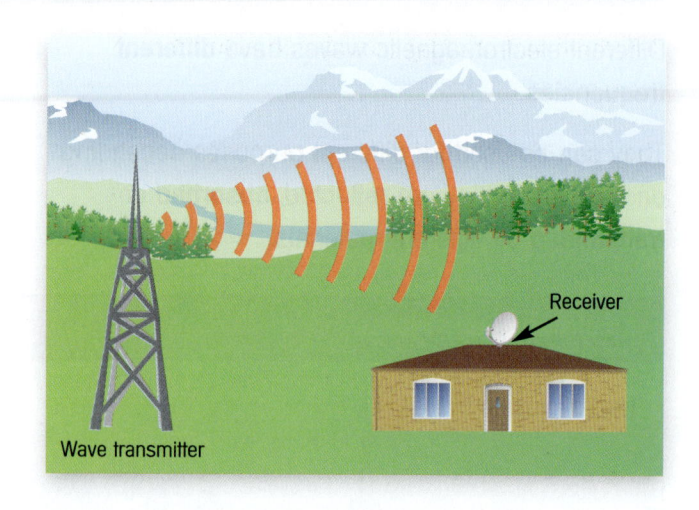

Analogue Signals

In amplitude modulation or frequency modulation (AM or FM) the amplitude or frequency of the carrier wave is changed by the input signal.

With frequency modulation the input signal causes the frequency of the carrier wave to change.

With amplitude modulation the input signal causes the amplitude of the carrier wave to change.

In both of these cases, the signal is called an **analogue signal** because it varies in exactly the same way as the information it's carrying. Analogue signals can have almost any value.

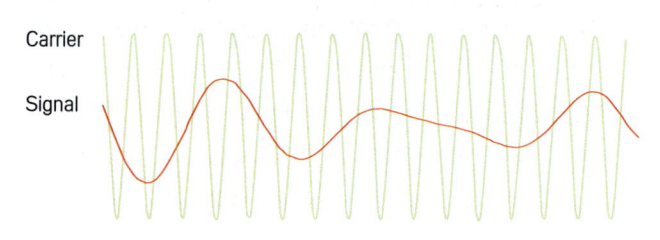

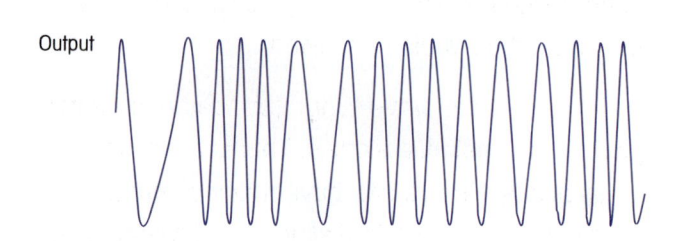

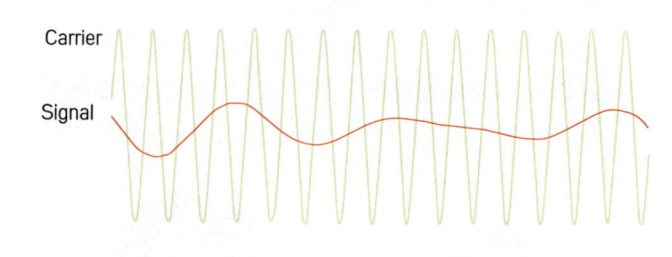

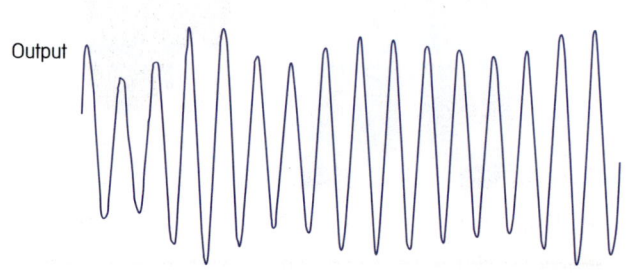

The Wave Model of Radiation

Digital Signals

Information, including sound, can also be transmitted **digitally**.

The signal is converted into a digital code that uses just two symbols (0 and 1) which can then be transmitted as a series of short bursts of waves called **pulses** (0 = no pulse, i.e. off, 1 = pulse, i.e. on).

When the digital signal is received, the pulses are decoded to produce a copy of the original sound wave.

Benefits of Digital Signals

Both digital and analogue signals…
- become weaker (their amplitude becomes smaller) as they travel so they may have to be **amplified** at selected intervals
- can pick up random variations, called **noise**, which reduce the quality of the sound.

When a signal is amplified, any noise which has been picked up is also amplified.

Digital signals can travel long distances at a **higher quality** than analogue signals. This is because…
- **analogue signals** can have many different values so it's hard to distinguish between noise and the original signal. This means that noise can't be completely removed.
- **digital signals** only have two states, on (1) or off (0), so they can still be recognised despite any noise that's picked up. This means that any **interference** can be removed.

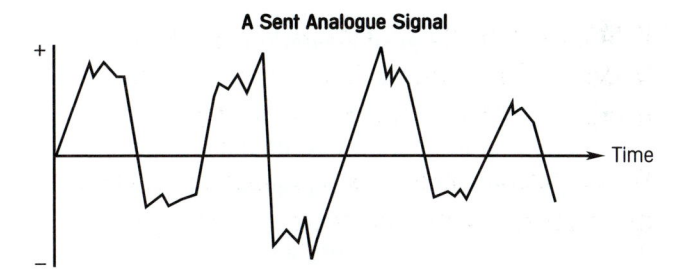

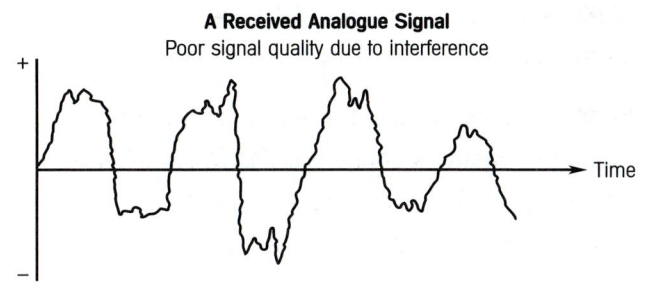

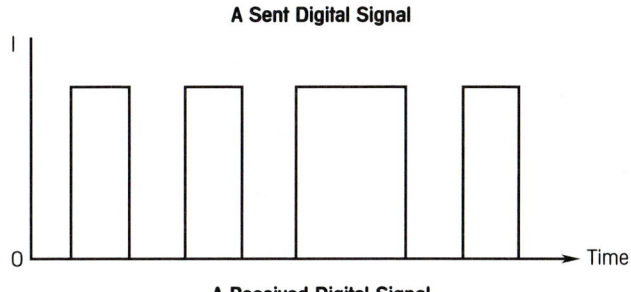

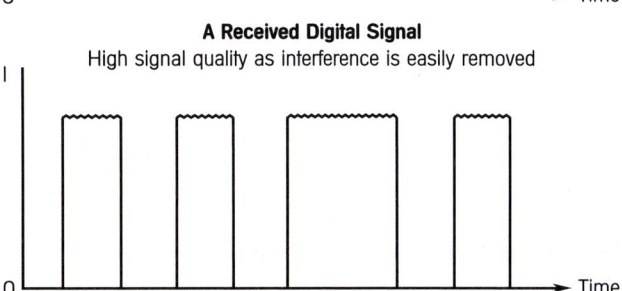

A Sent Analogue Signal

A Received Analogue Signal
Poor signal quality due to interference

A Sent Digital Signal

A Received Digital Signal
High signal quality as interference is easily removed

Key Words
Amplitude • Analogue • Digital • Frequency • Interference • Modulation

Module P6 Summary

Types of Waves

Waves = Regular patterns of disturbance that transfer energy from one point to another without transferring particles of matter.

There are two types of wave:
- Longitudinal.
- Transverse.

Longitudinal waves ➡ Particles vibrate to and fro.

Transverse waves ➡ Particles vibrate up and down.

Wave Features

Amplitude = Maximum disturbance caused by a wave.

Wavelength = Distance between corresponding points on two adjacent disturbances.

Frequency = Number of waves produced in one second. Measured in hertz.

If a wave travels at a constant speed…
- **increasing** frequency, **decreases** wavelength
- **decreasing** frequency, **increases** wavelength.

If a wave has a constant frequency…
- **increasing** wave speed, **increases** wavelength
- **decreasing** wave speed, **decreases** wavelength.

Wave speed (metre per second, m/s) = Frequency (hertz, Hz) × Wavelength (metre, m)

where v is wave speed, f is frequency and λ is wavelength

$$v = f \times \lambda$$

Behaviour of Waves

Refraction = Waves change direction when they pass between one medium and another.

Diffraction = Waves spread out from the edges when they pass an obstacle or through a narrow gap.

Reflection = Waves are reflected when a barrier is placed in their path.

Light

Light is reflected when it strikes a surface.

Incident ray = Light travelling **towards** a surface.

Reflected ray = Light travelling **away** from a surface.

Light…
- changes direction when it passes between one medium and another
- continues straight on when it meets a boundary at 90°.

Total internal reflection = Light is reflected when the angle of refraction is greater than 90° as it can't escape from the medium.

Module P6 Summary

Interference

Constructive interference = Two waves arrive in step and reinforce each other.

Destructive interference = Two waves arrive out of step and cancel each other out.

Interference pattern – caused when the light from one ray is either in step or out of step with the other ray.

Electromagnetic Radiation

Electromagnetic radiations form the **electromagnetic spectrum**.

Visible spectrum = The only part of the electromagnetic spectrum that can be seen.

Colours have…
- different frequencies
- different wavelengths.

Colours are refracted by different amounts as they pass through a prism:
- Red light ➡ Refracted the least.
- Violet light ➡ Refracted the most.

Photons = packets of energy.

HT Intensity of beam depends on **amount of energy** carried by each photon.

Electromagnetic waves can travel through empty space but sound waves need a medium to travel through.

Different electromagnetic waves have different **frequencies**.

Radio waves and microwaves ➡ Travel through Earth's atmosphere and space.

Light waves and infrared waves ➡ Travel through optical fibres.

Modulation

Modulation – makes a wave vary in amplitude or frequency to create a variation in the original wave.

The pattern of variation is decoded by a receiver to reproduce original sound.

Digital and Analogue Signals

Analogue signals = Vary in exactly the same way as the information they carry. Can have many different values.

Digital signals = Uses two symbols (0 = off and 1 = on) which can be transmitted as a series of pulses.

Digital signals can travel long distances at a higher quality than analogue signals because interference can be removed.

Module P6 Practice Questions

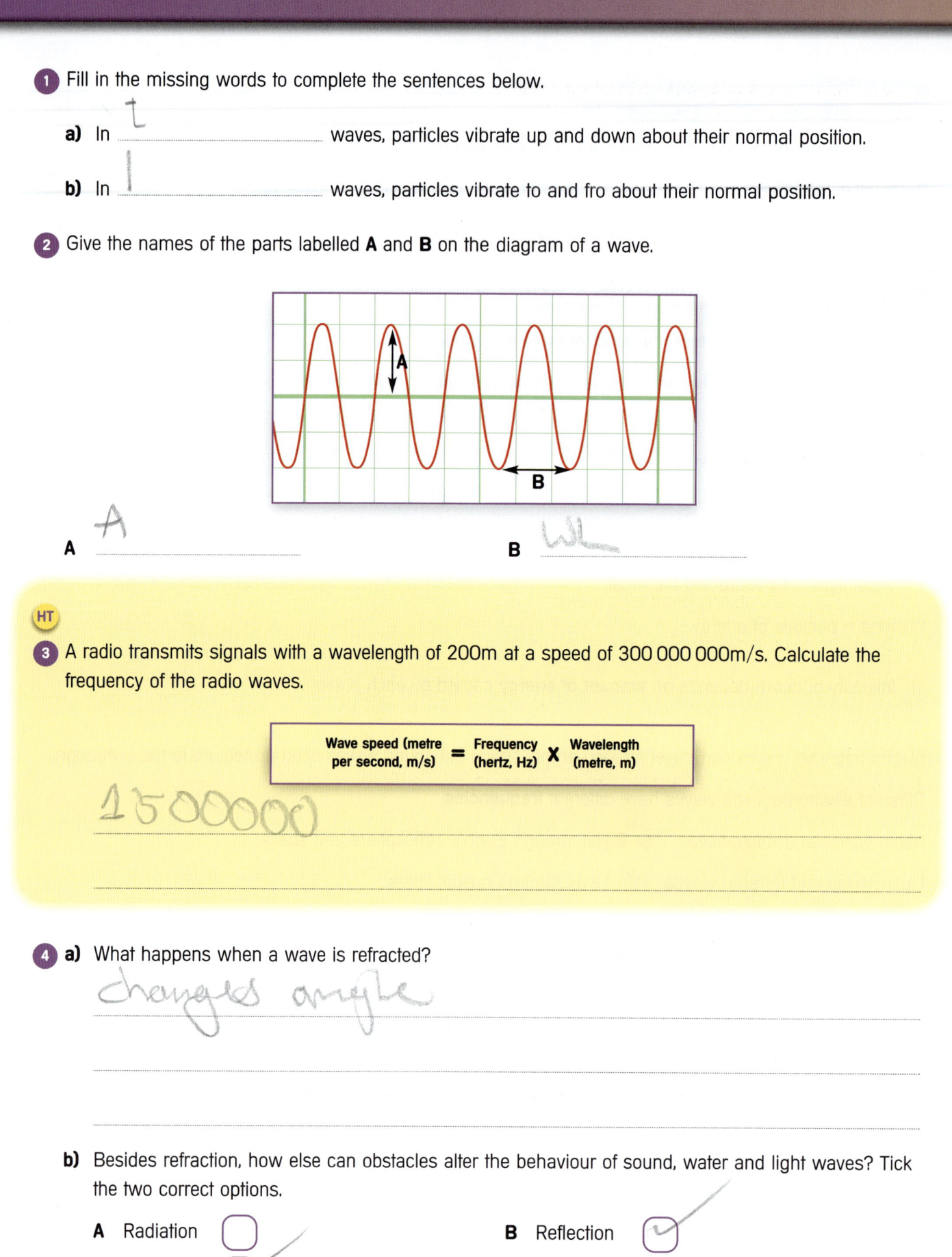

1 Fill in the missing words to complete the sentences below.

a) In ~~t~~ .... waves, particles vibrate up and down about their normal position.

b) In ~~l~~ .... waves, particles vibrate to and fro about their normal position.

2 Give the names of the parts labelled **A** and **B** on the diagram of a wave.

A *A*

B *wl...*

HT

3 A radio transmits signals with a wavelength of 200m at a speed of 300 000 000m/s. Calculate the frequency of the radio waves.

Wave speed (metre per second, m/s) = Frequency (hertz, Hz) × Wavelength (metre, m)

1500000

4 a) What happens when a wave is refracted?

changes angle

b) Besides refraction, how else can obstacles alter the behaviour of sound, water and light waves? Tick the two correct options.

A Radiation ☐
B Reflection ✓
C Diffraction ✓
D Modulation ☐

Module P6 Practice Questions

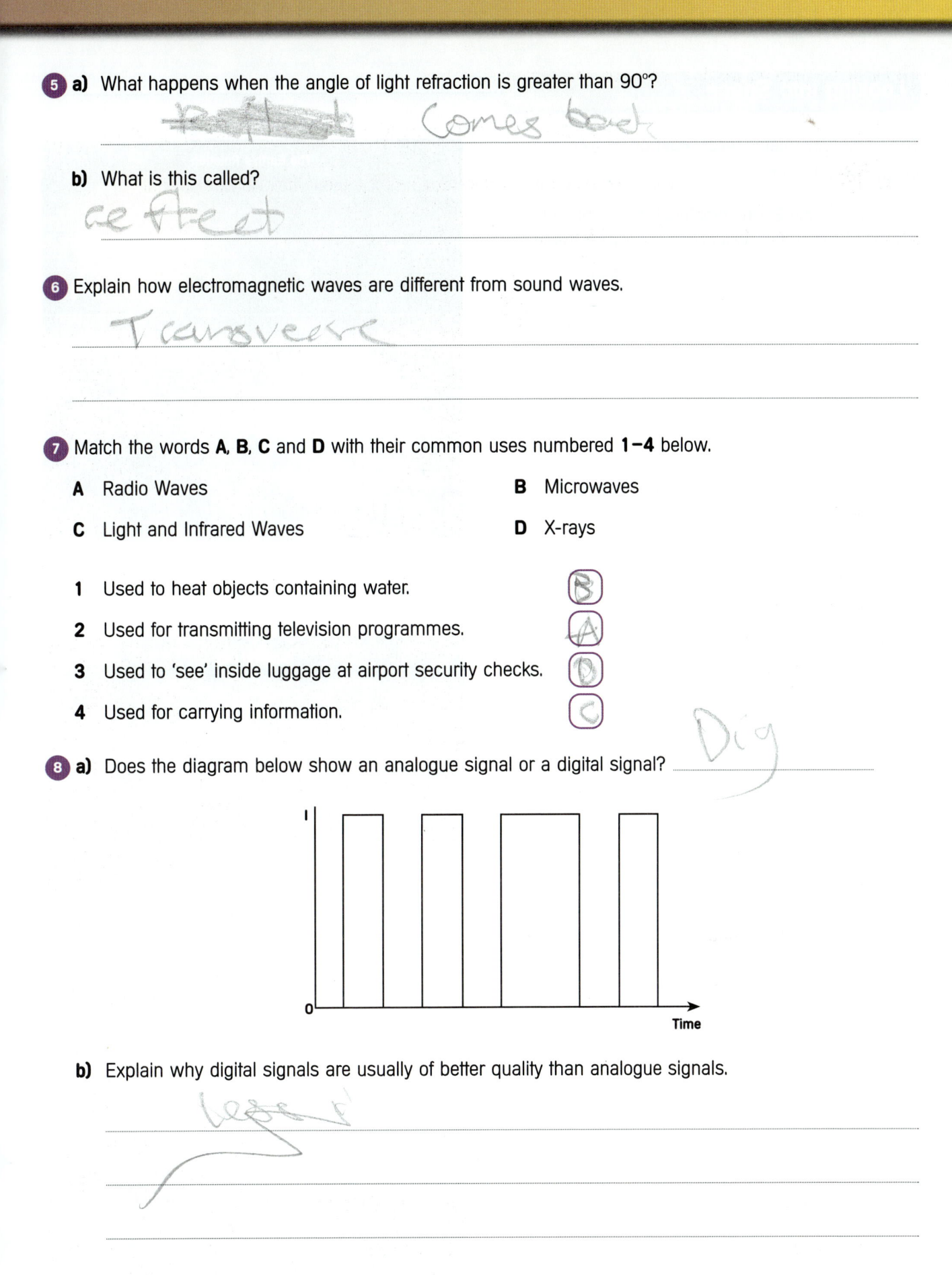

5 a) What happens when the angle of light refraction is greater than 90°?

comes back

b) What is this called?

reflect

6 Explain how electromagnetic waves are different from sound waves.

Transverse

7 Match the words **A**, **B**, **C** and **D** with their common uses numbered **1–4** below.

- **A** Radio Waves
- **B** Microwaves
- **C** Light and Infrared Waves
- **D** X-rays

1. Used to heat objects containing water. — B
2. Used for transmitting television programmes. — A
3. Used to 'see' inside luggage at airport security checks. — D
4. Used for carrying information. — C

8 a) Does the diagram below show an analogue signal or a digital signal? *Dig*

b) Explain why digital signals are usually of better quality than analogue signals.

Further Physics, Observing the Universe

Looking into Space

The Earth fully rotates **west–east** on its axis once in just under 24 hours.

We can't feel the Earth spinning, but it is this rotation that makes the stars **appear** to move **east–west** across the sky once in just under 24 hours.

The Sun, planets and Moon also appear to travel east–west across the sky. Their motion, and the time they take to cross the sky, is affected by their relevant orbits. The Sun appears to travel across the sky once every 24 hours.

HT Stars appear to travel east–west across the sky in 23 hours and 56 minutes.

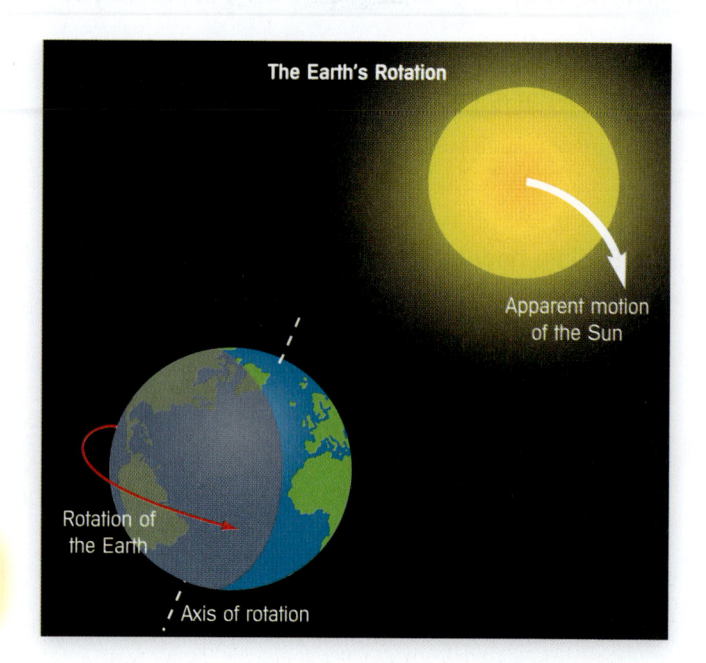

The Earth and the Sun

A **sidereal day** is the time it takes for the Earth to rotate 360° on its axis. A **solar day** is the time from noon on one day to noon on the next day, i.e. 24 hours.

Whilst the Earth rotates once on its axis, it also orbits the Sun. It is this **orbiting** movement that makes a sidereal day **shorter** than a solar day.

Look at the diagram:
1. The Sun is directly over a point on the Earth.
2. The Earth has rotated 360°, but as it's also orbiting the Sun, the Sun is no longer directly overhead.
3. The Earth has had time to rotate a bit more so the Sun is now directly overhead, making the solar day longer than the sidereal day.

HT A sidereal day is 4 minutes shorter than a solar day.

Key Words
Sidereal day • Solar day

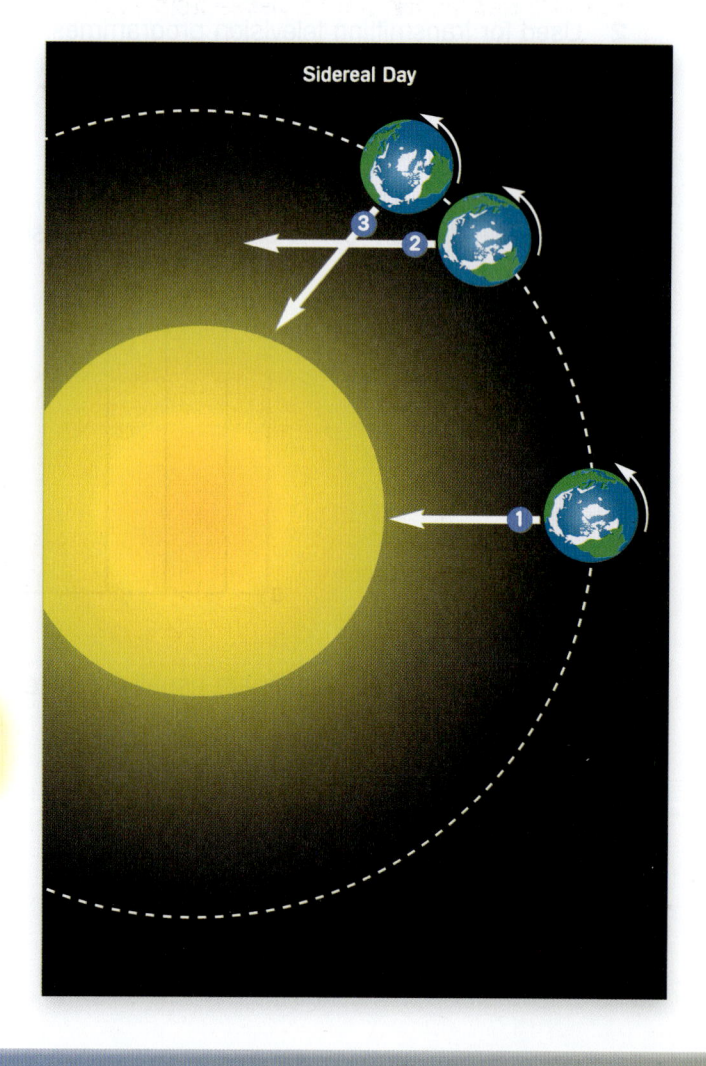

Further Physics, Observing the Universe

The Position of the Stars

The Earth orbits around the Sun. So, an observer looking at the night sky from the Earth can see different stars at different times of the year. The stars that can be seen will depend on the Earth's position in relation to the Sun's position.

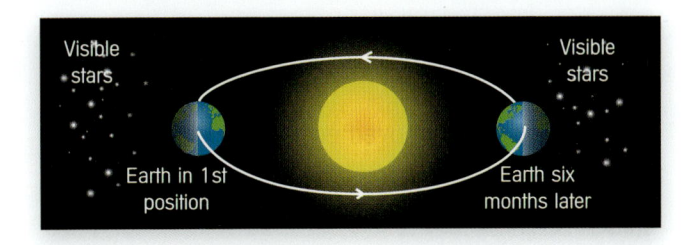

Plotting Astronomical Objects

The position of an astronomical object can be measured in terms of **angles** as seen from the Earth. The angles of **declination** and **ascension** describe the positions of the stars relative to a fixed point on the equator.

A star with a…

- **positive declination** will be visible from the **northern hemisphere**
- **negative declination** will be visible from the **southern hemisphere**.

The Planets

Mercury, Venus, Mars, Saturn and Jupiter are planets that can be seen from Earth with the naked eye.

From Earth, the planets look similar to stars. But, the planets change their positions in complicated patterns when compared to the background of fixed stars.

(HT) We can see how the planets change their positions by using observations of **Venus** as an example.

Venus is closer to the Sun than the Earth, so it orbits the Sun more quickly than the Earth does.

If Venus is observed over a long enough period of time (e.g. one month), it can be seen to **move compared** to the **background stars**.

1. When Venus is on the same side of the Sun as the Earth, it looks like it's travelling in one direction against the background stars.
2. When Venus is on the other side of the Sun to Earth, it looks like it's travelling in the opposite direction.

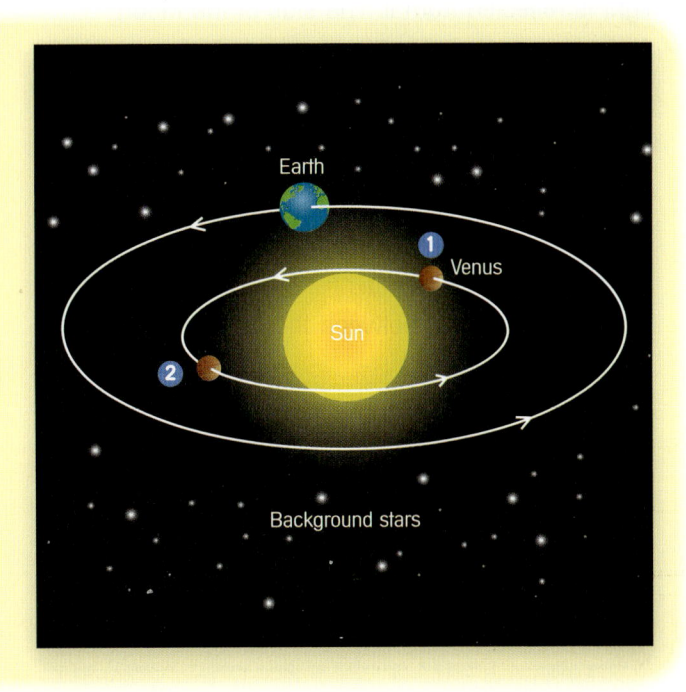

Further Physics, Observing the Universe

The Earth and the Moon

Whilst the Earth is rotating on its axis, the Moon is orbiting the Earth in the same direction.

Due to this orbiting movement, the Moon **appears** to travel **east–west** across the sky in a little over 24 hours.

For example, imagine you saw the Moon directly above you at a certain time one night. If you looked up again after one complete rotation of the Earth, the Moon wouldn't yet be directly above you. This is because the Earth's rotation would not yet have caught up with the Moon's new orbital position.

HT The Moon appears to travel east–west across the sky in 24 hours and 49 minutes.

Moon directly above point on Earth

24 hours later, the Earth has rotated 360°, but the Moon has moved on

Just over 24 hours later, the Earth's rotation has caught up with the Moon

The Lunar Cycle

The **lunar cycle** describes the Moon's appearance during its 28-day orbit of the Earth. The Moon's shape during this orbit is due to the part of the Moon that is **visible** from Earth.

We are able to see the Moon because the Sun's light is reflected from it. The side of the Moon **facing away** from the Sun appears **dark**, and the side **facing towards** the Sun appears **light**.

During the Moon's orbit around the Earth we can see different faces of the Moon:
- dark face (new Moon)
- light face (full Moon)
- all the points in between the new Moon and the full Moon.

The Orbit of the Moon

How the Moon is Seen from the Earth

Key Words

Eclipse • Ecliptic

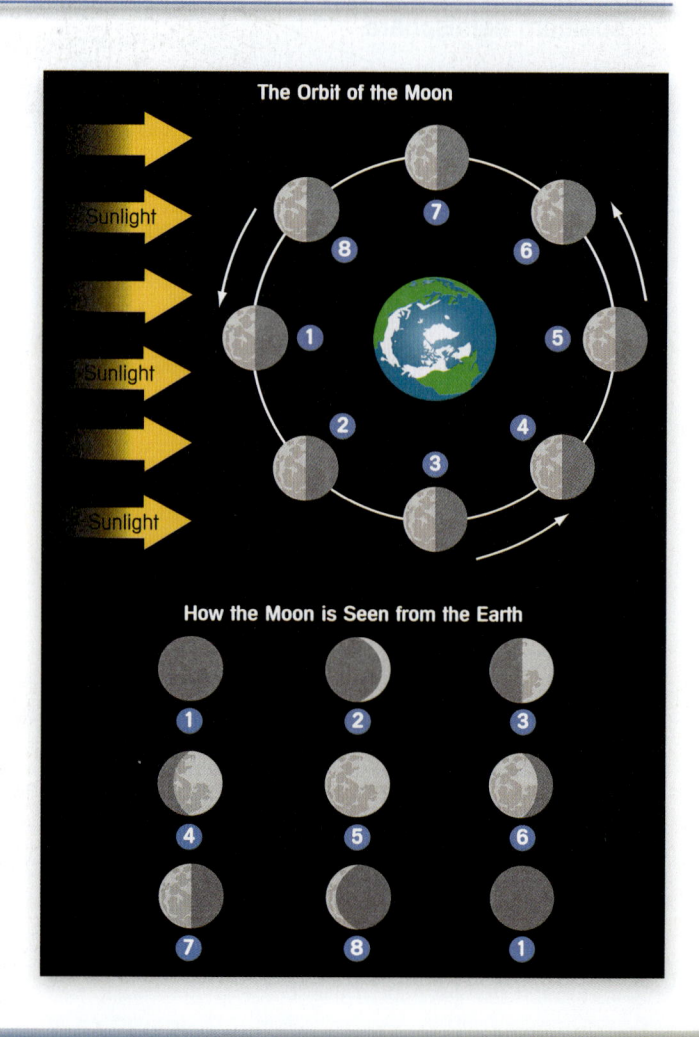

78

Further Physics, Observing the Universe

Solar Eclipses

A **solar eclipse** occurs when the **Moon passes** between the **Earth** and the **Sun**. This can happen during a new Moon and it results in the Moon casting **a shadow** on the Earth.

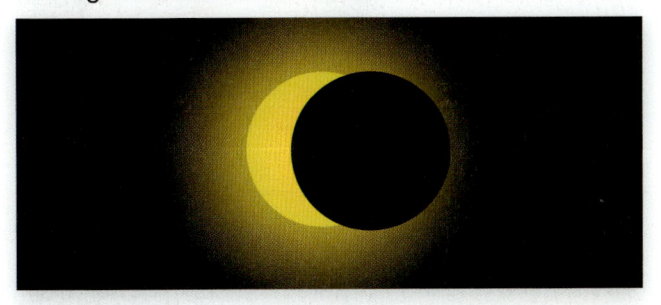

A **total solar eclipse** occurs when the Moon is directly in front of the Sun and completely obscures the Earth's view of the Sun.

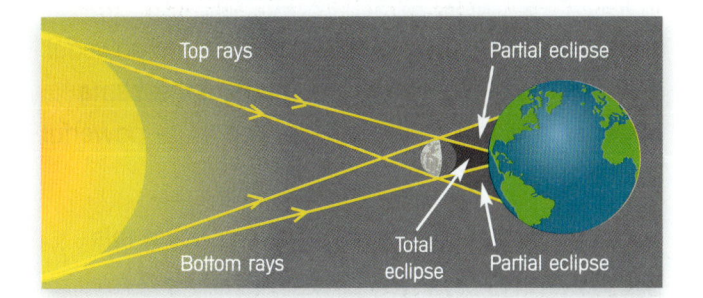

Lunar Eclipses

A **lunar eclipse** occurs when the **Earth** is between the **Sun** and the **Moon**. This results in the Earth casting **a shadow** on the Moon.

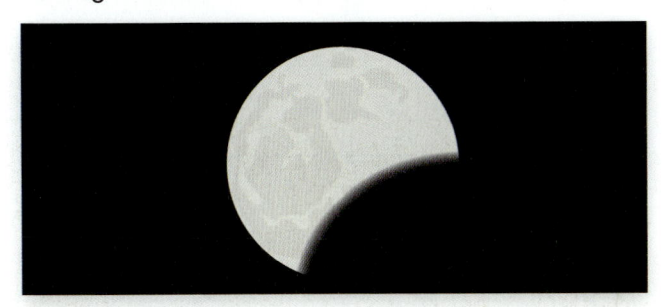

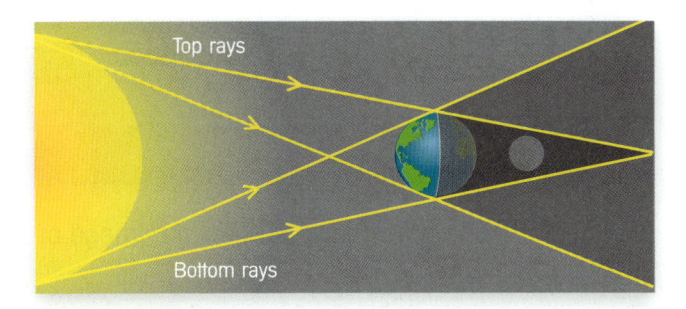

HT Frequency of Eclipses

Eclipses don't occur every month because the Moon doesn't orbit the Earth in the same plane as the Earth orbits the Sun. (The Moon's orbit is inclined 5° to that of the Earth's.)

So, an eclipse can only occur when the Moon passes through the **ecliptic** (the apparent path the Sun traces out along the sky). This is more likely to occur when the Moon is to the **side of the Earth**, rather than **between** the Earth and the Sun.

There are between 2 and 5 solar eclipses every year, but a total eclipse will only occur roughly every 18 months.

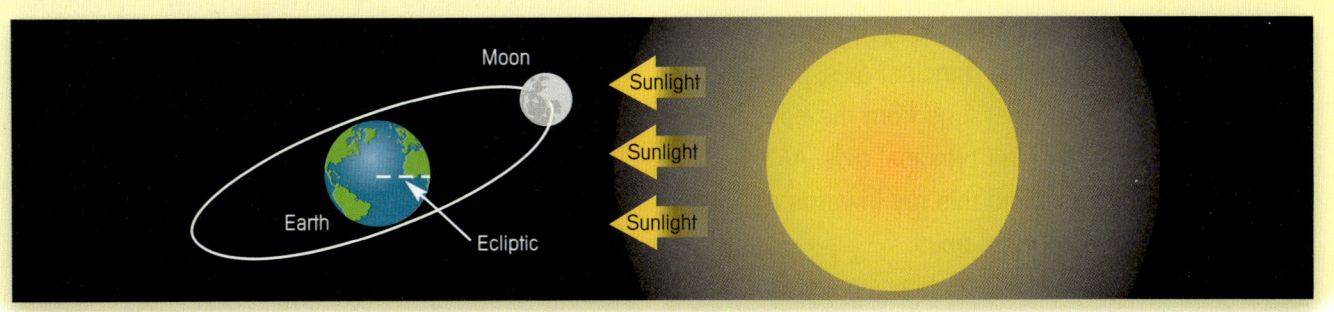

79

Further Physics, Observing the Universe

Convex Lenses

A **convex** (or converging) lens bends rays of light **inwards** as they pass through the lens. If the rays of light entering the lens are parallel, the rays will be brought to a **focus** at the focal point.

The greater the curvature of a lens, the more powerful it will be. So, if two lenses are made of the **same material**, a highly curved lens will be more powerful than a flatter lens.

You can calculate the power of a lens using this formula:

$$\text{Power (dioptre)} = \frac{1}{\text{Focal length (metre)}}$$

Example
If a convex lens has a focal length of 10cm, calculate its power.

$$\text{Power} = \frac{1}{\text{Focal length}} = \frac{1}{0.1\text{m}} = \textbf{10 dioptres}$$

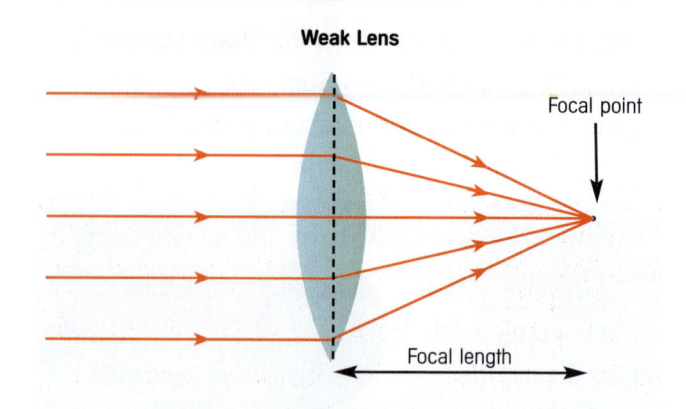

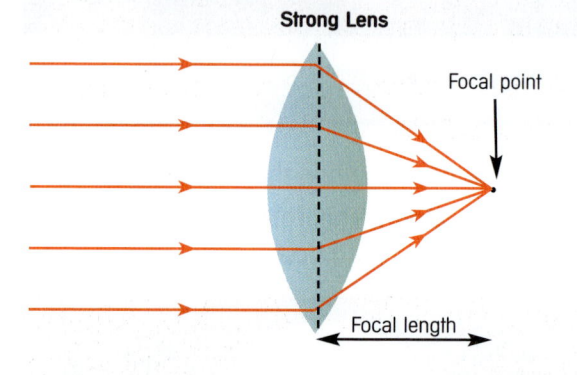

Weak Lens — Focal point, Focal length

Strong Lens — Focal point, Focal length

Ray Diagrams

Ray diagrams are drawn to show how the image of an object would be formed.

1. Draw a ray line (Ray 1) that runs from the top of the object parallel to the principal axis. At the middle of the lens, bend this ray inwards so it passes through the focal point (F).
2. Draw a second ray (Ray 2) that runs from the top of the object straight through the centre of the lens as it crosses the principal axis.
3. Draw a third ray (Ray 3) that runs from the top of the object through the focal point on the same side as the object. When the ray hits the centre of the lens, bend it to travel parallel to the principal axis.
4. If the object crosses the principal axis, draw another ray (Ray 4) that runs from the bottom of the object parallel to the principal axis. At the middle of the lens, bend this ray inwards so it passes through the focal point.
5. The image is formed where the rays meet.

You need to be able to draw ray diagrams for the formation of **real images** from a...
- **distant point** source
- **distant extended** source (the image produced will be **inverted** and **smaller**).

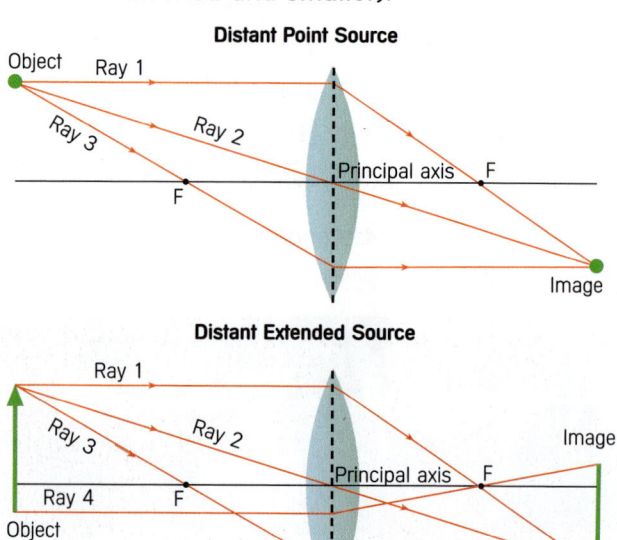

Distant Point Source

Distant Extended Source

Further Physics, Observing the Universe

Telescopes

Objects in space are so far away that rays of light from them seem to be parallel. So, we draw the rays of light entering telescopes as parallel rays.

A **simple refracting telescope** is made from two converging lenses of different powers. The **eyepiece lens** is a higher power lens than the **objective lens**.

An **astronomical telescope** normally uses a **concave mirror** for the objective lens instead of a **convex lens**. This allows them to be larger, which means they can collect more light.

Concave mirrors reflect rays of parallel light and bring them to a focus.

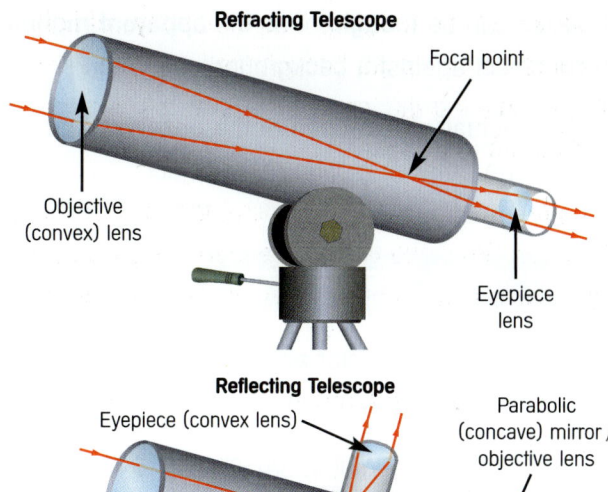

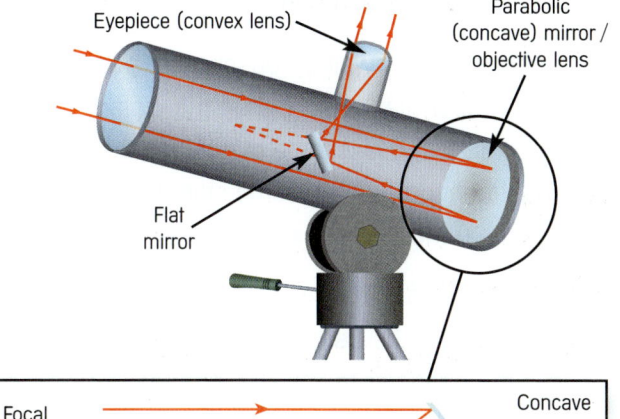

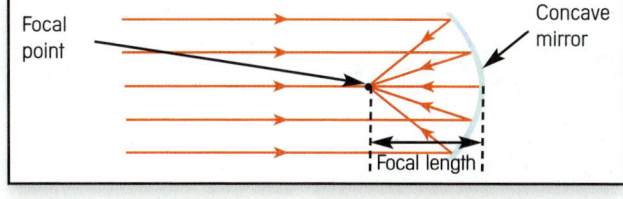

Key Words
Angular magnification • Focal point • Real image

HT Angular Magnification

The image of a **distant magnified object** will appear closer than the object. So, the angle made by ray lines entering the eye is greater.

This increase in angle is called the **angular magnification** and makes the image appear bigger / closer.

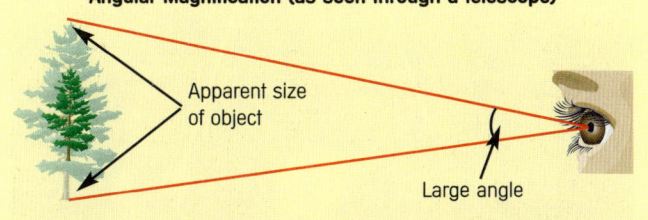

You can calculate the angular magnification of a telescope using this formula:

$$\text{Magnification} = \frac{\text{Focal length of objective lens}}{\text{Focal length of eyepiece lens}}$$

Example
The objective lens of a telescope has a focal length of 10m, and the eyepiece has a focal length of 2m. Calculate the magnification.

$$\text{Magnification} = \frac{\text{Focal length of objective lens}}{\text{Focal length of eyepiece lens}}$$
$$= \frac{10m}{2m}$$
$$= \times 5$$

Further Physics, Observing the Universe

Parallax

Parallax can be **thought** of as the **apparent motion** of an object against a background.

But, it's actually the **motion of the observer** that causes the parallax motion of an object.

A simple way to observe parallax is if you hold your hand out in front of you with your thumb sticking up and alternately close one eye then the other. Although your thumb appears to move, in reality you are just looking at it from a **different angle**.

Measuring Distance Using Parallax

Parallax can make a star **appear to move** in relation to the other stars in the course of a year.

In the diagram below, if an observer at **position ①** looks at a near star compared to the distant background, it **appears** to be at **position B**. But, if the observer then looks at the same star six months later, (**position ②**) the star **appears** to be at **position A**.

It looks as though the star has moved, but it's actually the **movement** of the **Earth's orbit** around the Sun that causes the observer to see this 'change in position'.

The **parallax angle** (θ) of a star is **half the angle** moved against a **background of distant** stars in **6 months**.

An object that is further away from the Earth will have a smaller parallax angle than a closer object.

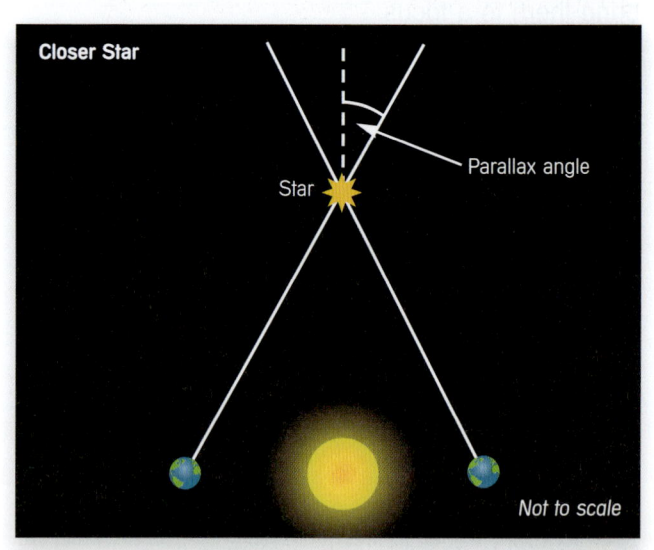

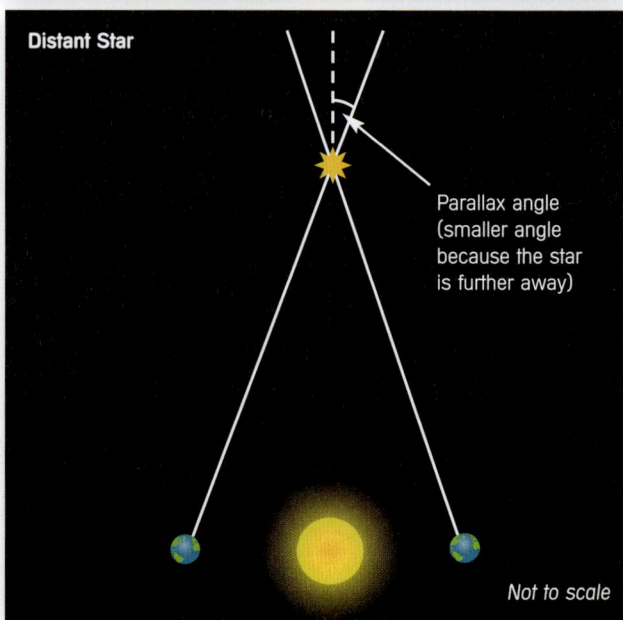

Closer Star — Parallax angle
Star
Not to scale

Parallax
A, B
Near star parallax motion
Near star
Parallax angle — θ
① ②
Earth's motion around the Sun
Not to scale

Distant Star
Parallax angle (smaller angle because the star is further away)
Not to scale

Further Physics, Observing the Universe

Using Parallax

Astronomers use parallax to measure **interstellar** distances using the unit **parsec** (**pc**). The typical interstellar distance between stars is a few parsecs.

A parsec is the **distance to a star** with a **parallax angle** of one **second of an arc**. It is of a similar size to a light year.

Astronomers can use the **megaparsec** (**Mpc**) to measure **intergalactic** distances even though these objects are so far away that the parallax angle is too small to measure.

For example, the nearest major galaxy, Andromeda, is 770 000 parsecs (0.77 Mpc) away.

You can calculate the distance in parsecs using this formula.

$$\text{Distance (parsecs)} = \frac{1}{\text{Parallax angle (arcseconds)}}$$

Example
The second-nearest star to Earth is *Proxima Centauri*. Astronomers found that it has a parallax angle of 0.77 arcseconds. Calculate its distance from the Earth.

$$\text{Distance} = \frac{1}{\text{Parallax angle}}$$
$$= \frac{1}{0.77 \text{ arcseconds}}$$
$$= \mathbf{1.3 \text{ parsecs}}$$

Measuring Distance Using Brightness

Astronomers can also measure the distance to stars by observing how **bright** the stars are.

In theory, this method sounds very simple, i.e. a **close** star will **appear brighter** than a **more distant** star. But, stars don't necessarily have the same intrinsic brightness (the amount of energy a star gives out).

A star's intrinsic brightness depends on its…
- size
- temperature.

A large or hot star will emit more light than a small or cool star. It may **appear brighter** even though it is **further away**.

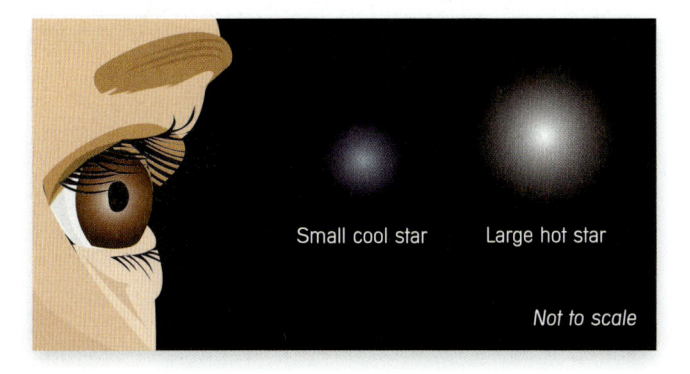

So, the observed brightness of a star depends on its…
- intrinsic brightness
- distance from the Earth.

A star with a **low intrinsic brightness** may **appear dull** even if it's very close to the Earth. And a star with a very **high intrinsic brightness** may **appear bright** even if it's very far from the Earth.

For example, the star Antares is 500 light years from the Earth. Although there are 100 000 stars closer to Earth than Antares, this star has an intrinsic brightness 10 000 times greater than that of the Sun and it's the 15th brightest star visible from Earth.

Small cool star   Large hot star

Not to scale

Key Words
Intrinsic brightness • Light year • Observed brightness • Parallax

Further Physics, Observing the Universe

Cepheid Variable Stars

A **Cepheid variable** star **doesn't** have a **constant** intrinsic brightness. It **pulses** and its brightness depends on the **frequency** of the pulses.

This changing frequency can be used to work out the **distance** to Cepheid variable stars.

By measuring the frequency of the pulses, astronomers can estimate the star's intrinsic brightness. The **distance** to the star can then be worked out if we know...
- how bright the star **really is**
- how bright the star **appears**.

The Curtis–Shapley Debate

In 1920, a great debate about the scale of the **Universe** took place between two prominent astronomers – Heber **Curtis** and Harlow **Shapley**.

Telescopes had revealed that the Milky Way contained lots of stars. This observation led to the realisation that the Sun was a star in the **Milky Way galaxy**.

Telescopes had also revealed many **fuzzy objects** in the night sky. These objects were originally called **nebulae** and they played a major role in the debate.

Curtis believed that the Universe consisted of many galaxies like our own, and the fuzzy objects were **distant galaxies**.

Shapley believed that the Universe contained only one big galaxy and the nebulae were nearby gas clouds **within the Milky Way**.

Edwin Hubble

In the mid-1920s, Edwin Hubble observed **Cepheid variables** in one **nebula** and found that the nebula was **much further away** than any star in the Milky Way.

This observation provided the evidence that the observed nebula was a **separate galaxy**. This supported Curtis' idea that the Universe contains many different galaxies.

Observations of many Cepheid variables have shown that most nebulae are distant galaxies.

This has allowed astronomers to measure the distance to these galaxies, and so determine the **scale of the Universe**.

Further Physics, Observing the Universe

The Hubble Constant

By observing Cepheid variable stars in distant galaxies, Edwin Hubble discovered that the Universe was **expanding**, in fact the **further away** a star was the **faster** it was **moving away**.

Cepheid variable stars in distant galaxies have been used to accurately calculate the **Hubble constant** because we know how far away they are.

So, we can use **red shift** to find out how fast they are moving away (their **speed of recession**).

Astronomers can now use the Hubble constant and red shift data to calculate the distance to other galaxies.

The speed of recession can be calculated using this formula:

$$\text{Speed of recession (km/s)} = \text{Hubble constant } (s^{-1}) \text{ or } (km\ s^{-1}\ Mpc^{-1}) \times \text{Distance (km) or (Mpc)}$$

Example 1
A galaxy is a distance of 3×10^{20} km from Earth. If the Hubble constant is $2.33 \times 10^{-18}\ s^{-1}$, calculate the speed of recession.

Speed of recession = Hubble constant × Distance

$= (2.33 \times 10^{-18}\ s^{-1}) \times (3 \times 10^{20}\ km)$

= 700 km/s

Example 2
A galaxy is a distance of 10 megaparsecs from Earth. If the Hubble constant is $70\ km\ s^{-1}\ Mpc^{-1}$, calculate the speed of recession.

Speed of recession = $70\ km\ s^{-1}\ Mpc^{-1} \times 10\ Mpc$

= 700 km/s

N.B. The speed of recession is the same in both examples. Example 1 uses distance in km and the Hubble constant in s^{-1}. Example 2 uses the astronomical unit of megaparsecs.

HT Example 3
Data from an observed galaxy gives the galaxy a speed of recession of 490 km/s. Calculate the distance to the galaxy in both kilometres and megaparsecs.

Hubble constant = $70\ km\ s^{-1}\ Mpc^{-1}$ or $2.33 \times 10^{-18}\ s^{-1}$)

$$\text{Distance} = \frac{\text{Speed of recession}}{\text{Hubble constant}}$$

$$\text{Distance (km)} = \frac{490\ km/s}{2.33 \times 10^{-18}}$$

= 2.1×10^{20} km

$$\text{Distance (Mpc)} = \frac{490\ km/s}{70\ km\ s^{-1}\ Mpc^{-1}}$$

= 7 Mpc

Example 4
A nearby galaxy is 0.77 Mpc from Earth and has a speed of recession of 54 km/s. What is the Hubble constant?

$$\text{Hubble constant} = \frac{\text{Speed of recession}}{\text{Distance}}$$

$$= \frac{54\ km/s}{0.77\ Mpc}$$

= $70.1\ km\ s^{-1}\ Mpc^{-1}$

Key Words
Cepheid variable • Frequency • Galaxy • Nebulae • Red shift • Universe

Further Physics, Observing the Universe

Pressure and Volume

Fluid pressure is caused by **particles** in a fluid **moving about**. When a particle collides with an object it exerts a force. This force is felt as pressure.

The amount of pressure depends on…
- the number of collisions per second
- the momentum of the particles.

As the volume of a fluid is reduced, the particles have less room to move about. So, they collide with each other more often, **increasing the pressure**.

Gas Inside a Piston

Pressure and Temperature

If a fluid is **heated up**, the particles move around **faster**. This increases their momentum and the force they exert when they collide with each other.

This could have two effects:
1. **Increase the volume** (by pushing the piston up).
2. **Increase the pressure** (if the volume is kept fixed).

N.B. *This effect also works in reverse, i.e. compressing a gas will cause it to increase in temperature.*

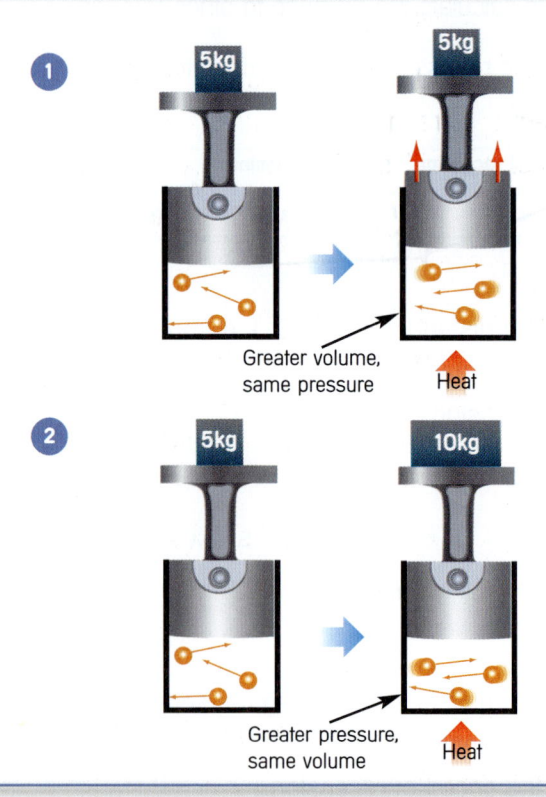

Absolute Zero

As the **temperature** of a gas is **reduced**, the particles in the gas move **slower** and the **pressure falls**.

The particles eventually stop moving altogether. At this point the particles have no more energy to lose and the temperature can't get any lower. This occurs at -273°C, otherwise known as absolute zero.

Absolute temperature is a measure of temperature starting at absolute zero and is measured in **Kelvins (K)**.

To convert from…
- Kelvin into degrees Celsius, subtract 273
- degrees Celsius into Kelvin, add 273.

Example

a) Convert 400K to °C.
   T(°C) = 400 − 273 = **127°C**

b) Convert 100°C to K.
   T(K) = 100 + 273 = **373K**

Further Physics, Observing the Universe

The Structure of a Star

A star has three main parts:
- The **core** is the hottest part of the star where fusion takes place.
- The **convective zone** is where energy is transported to the surface by convection currents.
- The **photosphere** is where energy is radiated into space.

Like all hot objects, stars emit a continuous range of **electromagnetic radiation**. They emit radiation of a…
- **high intensity**
- **high peak frequency** (i.e. frequency where most energy is emitted).

An object that is red hot emits most of its energy in the red frequency range. The frequency of light given off from a star provides evidence of how hot it is.

Structure of a Star

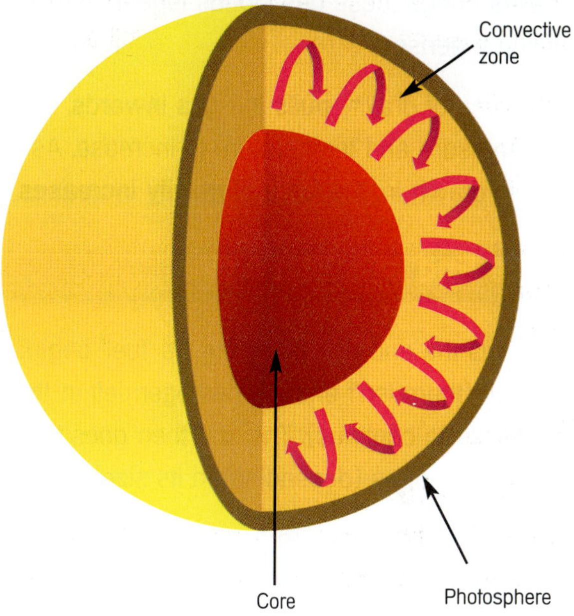

Convective zone

Core

Photosphere

Using a Star's Spectrum

The **removal** of electrons from an atom is called **ionisation**. The **movement** of electrons within the atom causes it to emit radiation of specific frequencies called **line spectra**. Different elements have characteristic line spectra.

Due to its high temperature, the spectrum from a star is continuous, apart from the spectral lines of the elements it contains (these lines are missing because they are absorbed).

By comparing a star's spectrum to emission spectra from elements, we can see which chemical elements the star contains.

For example, the diagrams opposite compare the emission spectrum for hydrogen and the absorption spectrum that would be seen from the Sun.

The Sun's spectrum is complex, indicating that it contains more than one element. But, by comparing the spectra we can see that the Sun contains hydrogen as well as some other elements (e.g. helium).

Hydrogen Spectrum

The Sun's Spectrum

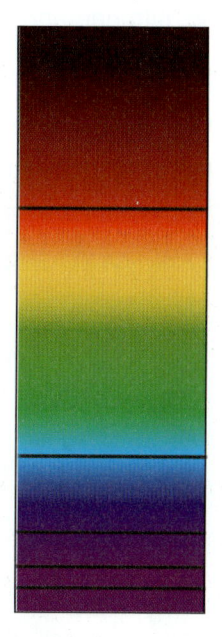

Key Words
Absolute zero • Force • Ionisation • Pressure • Radiation

Further Physics, Observing the Universe

The Beginning of a Star's Life

Stars begin as clouds of gas (mainly hydrogen). As gravity brings these gas clouds together, they become denser.

The force of gravity **pulls** the **gas inwards**, causing the pressure and temperature to increase. As more gas is drawn in, the force of **gravity increases**.

This compresses the gas so that it becomes hotter and denser, and forms a **protostar**.

Eventually, the temperature and pressure become so high that the hydrogen nuclei fuse into helium nuclei. Energy is released in this fusion process. The star is now a stable **main sequence star**.

The End of a Star's Life

Towards the end of a star's life, its 'fuel' begins to run out (there isn't enough hydrogen left in the core for fusion to continue). The star then goes through several changes (depending on its size).

When the core hydrogen has been used up, the star becomes cooler. Small stars like our Sun become **red giants**, while larger stars become **red supergiants**.

Red giants and red supergiants continue to release energy by fusing helium into larger nuclei such as carbon, nitrogen and oxygen.

Once the helium has been used up, red giants no longer have enough mass to compress the core and continue fusion. They shrink into hot **white dwarfs** that gradually cool.

Red supergiants have a much greater mass and higher core pressures than red giants, so fusion continues to produce larger nuclei, such as iron.

Once the core is mostly iron, the red supergiant explodes in a **supernova**, leaving behind a dense **neutron star** or a **black hole**.

The Life Cycle of a Star

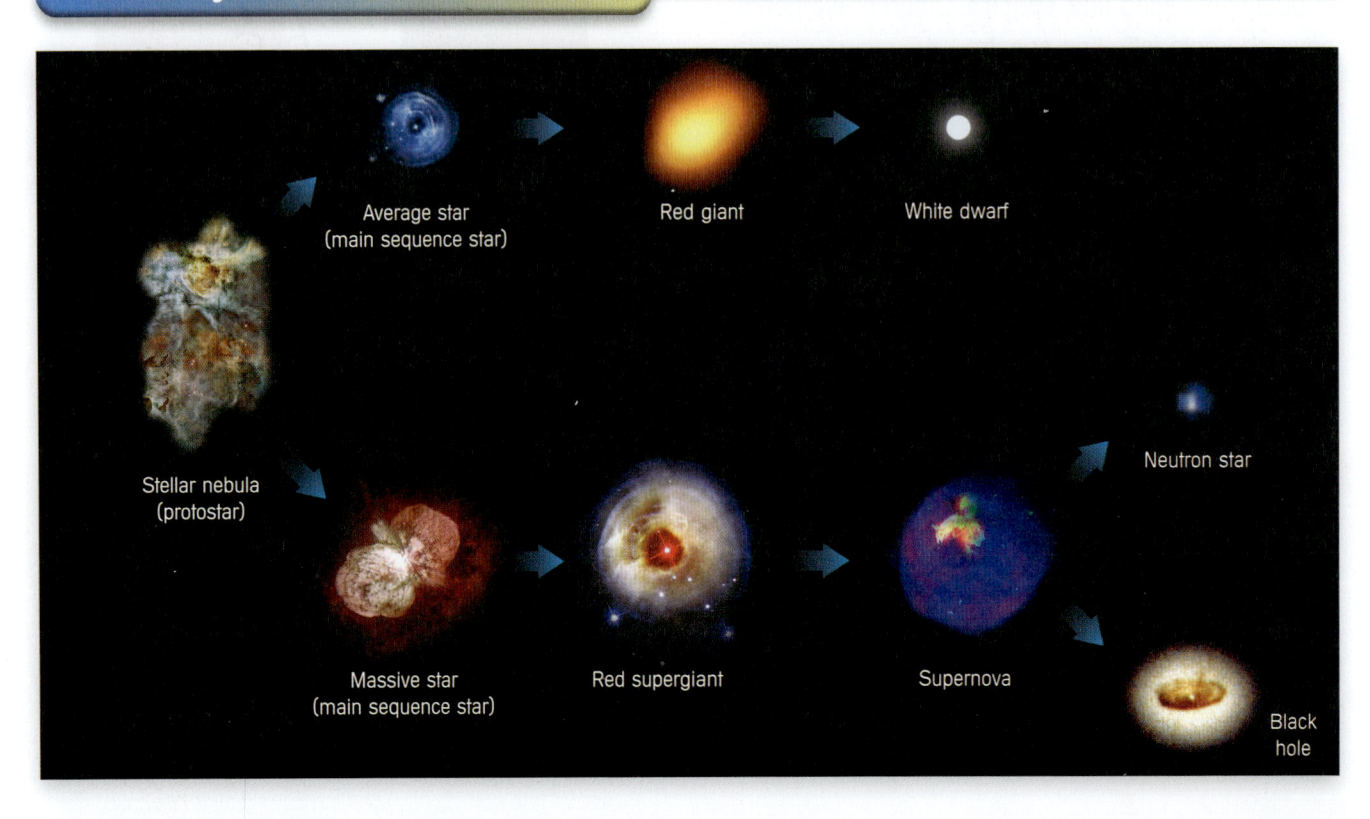

Further Physics, Observing the Universe

Alpha Particle Scattering Experiment

At the beginning of the 20th Century, discoveries about the nature of the atom and nuclear processes began to answer the mystery of the source of the Sun's energy.

In 1911, there was a ground-breaking experiment – the Rutherford-Geiger-Marsden alpha particle scattering experiment.

In this experiment, a thin **gold foil** was bombarded with alpha particles. The effect on the **alpha particles** was recorded and these observations provided the evidence for our current understanding of atoms.

Three observations were recorded:
- Most alpha particles were seen to **pass straight through** the gold foil.
- Some particles were **deflected** slightly.
- A few particles **bounced back** towards the source.

Particles passing through the foil indicated that gold atoms are composed of large amounts of space. The deflection and bouncing back of particles indicated that these alpha particles passed close to something positively charged within the atom and were repelled by it.

The Gold Foil Scattering Experiment

- Alpha particle
- Most particles passed straight through
- Some particles were deflected back
- Some particles were deflected slightly
- Gold atom

Conclusions of Experiment

The observations of this experiment brought Rutherford and Marsden to conclude the following points:
- Gold atoms, and therefore all atoms, consist largely of empty space with a small, dense core. They called this core the **nucleus**.
- The nucleus is positively charged.
- The **electrons** are arranged around the nucleus with a great deal of space between them.

We now know that the nucleus contains **positive protons** and **neutral neutrons** held together by the short-ranged **strong nuclear force**.

Protons normally **repel** each other (because they have the same charge), but this nuclear force is much stronger than the repulsive electrical force. So, when protons are close enough, the nuclear force takes over and the protons **fuse** into a larger nucleus.

This fusion process releases large amounts of energy and is the source of the Sun's power.

Key Words
Electron • Fusion • Gravity • Nucleus

Further Physics, Observing the Universe

Telescopes

As astronomers try to gather more evidence about the **Universe**, they need to examine objects that are a very long way from Earth.

These distant objects will often emit very faint or weak radiation. So, in order to pick up this radiation, larger, complex and more expensive telescopes need to be built.

Astronomers use different types of **ground-based** or **space-based** telescopes, including radio, optical and infrared.

Radio and Infrared Telescopes

Radio telescopes use a metal reflector to reflect radio waves onto a receiver. Radio waves aren't blocked by clouds or affected by weather, so radio telescopes are able to detect objects that are too cool to emit much visible or infrared light.

A large radio telescope is needed in order to produce good-quality images, but even then the images produced will not be as clear as ones produced by an optical telescope.

Infrared telescopes work much like optical telescopes. They have a better **resolution** than radio telescopes and can observe cooler objects that don't give off visible light.

But, because infrared light is easily absorbed by the Earth's atmosphere, these telescopes need to be…
- built at high altitude
- based in space.

HT Diffraction

Radiation is **diffracted** by the **aperture** of a telescope. To produce a sharp image, the aperture must be much larger than the wavelength of the radiation.

Large radio telescopes can detect weak radio waves. But, radio waves have a long wavelength affected by diffraction, so the image produced isn't very sharp.

Light has a very short wavelength. Optical telescopes have a much larger aperture than the light's wavelength, so they can produce a sharp image.

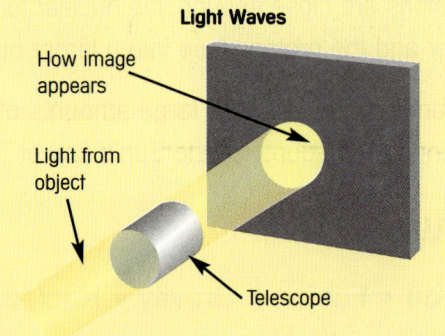

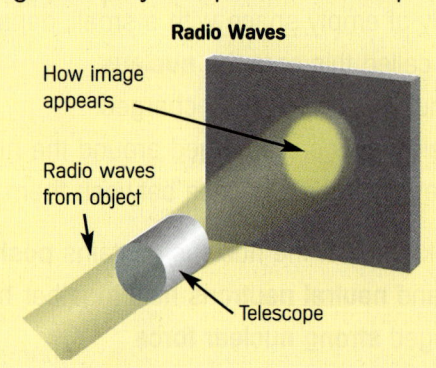

Light Waves

Radio Waves

Further Physics, Observing the Universe

Ground-Based Optical Telescopes

There are several locations of major astronomical observatories, for example, the...
- **Royal Observatory** in Greenwich (the largest refracting optical telescope in the UK)
- **Mauna Kea Observatories**, Hawaii (the largest optical reflecting telescopes in the world).

Astronomical factors will often influence the choice of a site. For example, Hawaii has proven an ideal location because of its...
- **high altitude** (there is less atmosphere above it to absorb the light from distant objects)
- **isolated location** (there is less pollution to interfere with the received signal)
- **equatorial location** (which gives it the best view of solar eclipses).

There are other factors that should be considered when planning, building, operating or closing down an observatory. For example...
- cost
- environmental and social impact near the observatory
- working conditions for employees.

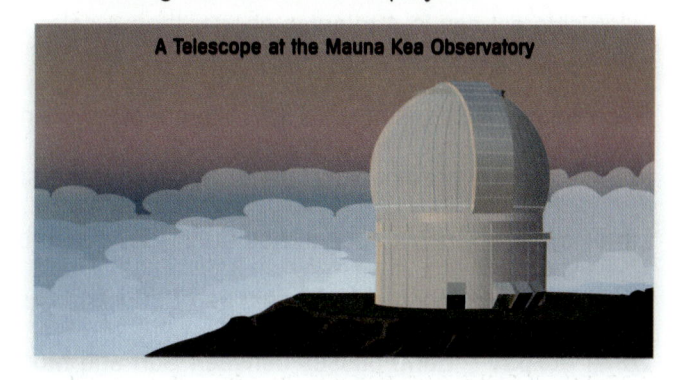

A Telescope at the Mauna Kea Observatory

Space-Based Telescopes

Space-based telescopes, e.g. the **Hubble telescope**, can obtain images of the Universe that can't be obtained in any other way.

Advantages of space telescopes include:
- They avoid the absorption and refraction effects of the Earth's atmosphere.
- They can use parts of the electromagnetic spectrum that the atmosphere absorbs.

Disadvantages of space telescopes include:
- They are very expensive to set up, maintain and repair.
- There are uncertainties associated with space programmes, e.g. launch delays.

Funding Developments in Science

Most of the big new telescopes are developed through **international co-operation**. There are several advantages to this kind of joint venture:
- The **cost** of building the telescopes is **shared**.
- **Expertise** can be **shared**.
- Astronomers can book time on telescopes in different countries, allowing them to see the stars on other sides of the Earth.

For example, the Gemini Observatory in Chile (which opened in 2002) was the result of shared work between Australia and six other countries.

These telescopes can be accessed...
- directly at the site
- through remote computer control (so astronomers don't have to travel to each telescope and can use it at convenient times)
- through the Internet (schools in the UK can access the Royal Observatory in this way).

Key Word
Universe

Module P7 Summary

Movement of Objects in Space

Stars, planets and the Moon appear to travel **east–west** across the sky.

Sidereal day – Time it takes the Earth to rotate 360°.

Solar day = 24 hours

> **HT** Stars appear to travel once across the sky in 23 hours 56 minutes.
> The Moon appears to travel once across the sky in 24 hours 49 minutes.
> A sidereal day is 4 minutes shorter than a solar day.

Earth rotates round the Sun ➡ Different stars seen at different times of year.

Planets change positions compared to background stars.

Lunar cycle = Moon's appearance during 28-day orbit of Earth.

Solar eclipse = Moon passes between Earth and Sun.

Lunar eclipse = Earth passes between Sun and Moon.

Parallax ➡ Thought of as apparent motion of object against background ➡ Caused by motion of observer.

Parallax angle of star = Half the angle moved against a background of distant stars in 6 months.

Parsec = Distance to a star with a parallax angle of one second of an arc.

Stars

Star's **intrinsic** brightness ➡ Size and temperature.

Star's **observed** brightness ➡ Intrinsic brightness and distance from Earth.

Cepheid variable star ➡ Pulses ➡ Varying brightness ➡ Used to work out distance.

Star has 3 main parts:
- **Core** = where fusion takes place.
- **Convective zone** = where energy is transported to surface.
- **Photosphere** = where energy is radiated into space.

Star's **spectrum** show the different elements it contains.

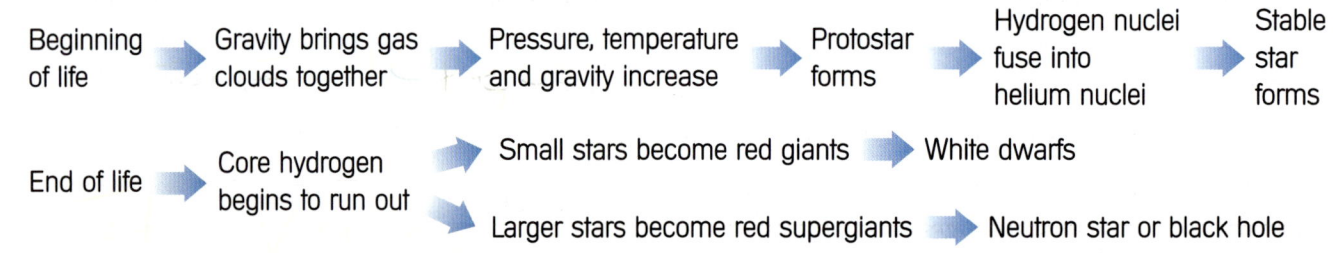

Beginning of life ➡ Gravity brings gas clouds together ➡ Pressure, temperature and gravity increase ➡ Protostar forms ➡ Hydrogen nuclei fuse into helium nuclei ➡ Stable star forms

End of life ➡ Core hydrogen begins to run out ➡ Small stars become red giants ➡ White dwarfs

Larger stars become red supergiants ➡ Neutron star or black hole

Module P7 Summary

Curtis–Shapley Debate

Fuzzy objects in the sky called nebulae:
- Curtis believed nebulae were distant galaxies.
- Shapley believed nebulae were gas clouds within our Galaxy.

Studying Cepheid variables provided evidence that nebulae were distant galaxies

Speed of recession (km/s)	=	Hubble constant (s^{-1}) ($km\ s^{-1}\ Mpc^{-1}$)	×	Distance (km) (Mpc)

Pressure, Temperature and Volume

Particles collide ➡ Force exerted ➡ Felt as pressure.

Volume of fluid reduced ➡ Pressure increases.

Fluid heated up ➡ Volume increases.
➡ Pressure increases (if volume is fixed).

Absolute temperature ➡ Measure of temperature starting at **absolute zero** (-273°C) ➡ Measured in Kelvins (K).

Kelvin converted into degrees Celsius = subtract 273. Degrees Celsius converted into Kelvin = add 273.

Alpha Particle Scattering Experiment

Gold foil bombarded with alpha particles ➡ Most particles passed straight through, some were deflected or bounced back.

Conclusions = Atoms have small, dense, positive core called **nucleus**. Electrons arranged around nucleus.

Telescopes

$$\text{Power (dioptre)} = \frac{1}{\text{Focal length (metre)}}$$

$$\text{Magnification} = \frac{\text{Focal length of objective lens}}{\text{Focal length of eyepiece lens}}$$

Telescopes can be **ground-based** or **space-based**.

International co-operation is beneficial to developing space technology.

HT Angular magnification ➡ Larger angle from distant, **magnified** object ➡ Object appears bigger/closer.

Radio ➡ Long wavelength ➡ Easily diffracted ➡ Fuzzy image

Light ➡ Short wavelength ➡ Not diffracted easily ➡ Sharp image

Module P7 Practice Questions

1 Explain the difference between a sidereal day and a solar day.

Sidereal is time for earth to turn 360°

2 The lunar cycle is caused by the shadow of the Earth falling on the moon. Is this statement **true** or **false**?

False (crossed out)

HT

3 How long does it take for the Moon to appear to travel once across the sky?

1:49

4 a) What happens to parallel rays of light as they pass through a convex lens? Sketch a diagram to illustrate your answer.

They are turned into a focal point

b) Calculate the power of a lens that has a focal length of 20cm.

5 dioptres

5 a) Use the words below to help you complete the following sentences:

parallax   larger   further   apparent   close

The _apparent_ motion of an object caused by the observer moving is called _parallax_. An object that is _closer_ to Earth will have a _larger_ parallax angle than an object that is _further_ from Earth.

b) If a star has a parallax angle of 0.1 arcseconds, calculate its distance from Earth in parsecs.

$\frac{1}{0.1} = 10$ pgc's

6 With regards to brightness, how does a Cepheid variable star differ from a normal star?

It varies

Module P7 Practice Questions

HT

7 A galaxy has a speed of recession of 2800km/s. If the hubble constant is 70km s⁻¹ Mpc⁻¹, calculate its distance from Earth.

$\frac{2800}{70}$ = 40 mpc

8 If a fluid is heated up, and the volume is kept fixed, what happens to the pressure? Tick the correct option.

- A It will stay the same
- B It will decrease
- C It will increase ✓
- D It will decrease, then increase

9 What name is given to the temperature at which all particles have stopped moving?

Absolute zero

10 Complete the table below:

Temperature (°Celsius)	Temperature (Kelvin)
20	a) 293
-100	b) 173
c) 227	500

11 Draw lines to link each part of a star to its correct description.

Convective zone	Where energy is transported to the surface by convection currents
Core	Where energy is radiated into space
Photosphere	The hottest part of the star

(Convective zone → convection currents; Core → hottest part; Photosphere → radiated into space)

12 When Rutherford and Marsden conducted their experiment, describe the three things that happened to the alpha particles as they bombarded the gold foil atoms.

a) Some passed through

b) Some deflected slightly

c) Some fully rebounded

Glossary of Key Words

Absolute zero – the lowest temperature possible.

Acceleration – the rate at which an object increases in speed.

Alpha – a radioactive particle made of 2 protons and 2 neutrons.

Alternating current – an electric current that changes direction of flow continuously.

Amplitude – the maximum disturbance caused by a wave.

Analogue – a signal that varies continuously in amplitude / frequency; can take any value.

Atom – the smallest part of an element that can enter into a chemical reaction.

Beta – a type of radioactive particle made of an electron.

Big Bang – a theory of how the Universe started.

Carbon cycle – the constant recycling of carbon by the processes in life, death and decay.

Cepheid variable – a star that has a changing intrinsic brightness.

Continental drift – the movement of continents being carried on tectonic plates.

Convection current – a stream of warm, moving fluid.

Current – the rate of flow of an electrical charge, measured in amperes (A).

Decomposer – an organism that breaks down other matter.

Deforestation – the destruction of forests by cutting down trees.

Diffraction – the spreading out of a wave as it passes an obstacle and expands into the region beyond the obstacle.

Digital – a signal that uses binary code to represent information; has two states: on (1) and off (0).

Direct current – an electric current that only flows in one direction.

Distance–time graph – a graph showing distance travelled against time taken; the gradient of the line represents speed.

Eclipse – the shadow cast by an object.

Efficiency – the useful energy output expressed as a percentage of total energy input.

Electromagnetic spectrum – a continuous arrangement that displays electromagnetic waves in order of increasing frequency.

Electron – a negatively charged subatomic particle that orbits the nucleus.

Element – a substance that consists of only one type of atom.

Energy transfer – the movement of energy from one place to another.

Erosion – the wearing away of the Earth's surface.

Focal point – the point at which all light rays parallel to the axis of the lens converge.

Force – a push or pull acting upon an object.

Frequency – the number of times that something happens in a set period of time; the number of times a wave oscillates in one second; measured in hertz.

Friction – the resistive force between two surfaces as they move over each other.

Fusion – the joining together of two or more atomic nuclei to form a larger atomic nucleus.

Galaxy – a collection of stars and planets in a solar system.

Gamma – a radioactive emission that is an electromagnetic wave.

Geohazard – any natural hazard associated with the Earth, e.g. an earthquake.

Glossary of Key Words

Global warming – the gradual increase in the average temperature on Earth.

Gradient – the steepness of the slope of a graph.

Gravity – a force of attraction between masses; the force that keeps objects orbiting larger objects.

Greenhouse effect – the process by which the Earth is kept warm by the atmosphere reflecting heat back down towards the Earth, preventing it from escaping into space.

Half-life – the time taken for half the radioactive atoms in a material to decay.

Instantaneous speed – the speed of an object at a particular point.

Interference – the effect created when two waves meet, either in step or out of step.

Intrinsic brightness – the brightness of a star, dependent on its size and temperature.

Ion – a positively or negatively charged particle formed when an atom, or group of atoms, loses or gains electrons.

Ionisation – the removal of electrons.

Irradiated – to be exposed to radioactive emissions.

Kinetic energy – the energy possessed by an object because of its movement.

Light speed – the speed at which light travels.

Light year – the distance light travels in one year.

Longitudinal – an energy-carrying wave in which the movement of the particles is in line with the direction in which the energy is being transferred.

Modulation – to change the amplitude or frequency of a carrier wave by adding a signal.

Momentum – a measure of state of motion of an object as a product of its mass and velocity.

Nebulae – interstellar clouds of dust, hydrogen gas and plasma; other galaxies in the making.

Neutron – a particle found in the nucleus of an atom that has no electrical charge.

Neutron star – the extremely dense remainder of some of the largest stars.

Nuclear fusion – the joining together of two or more atomic nuclei to form a larger atomic nucleus.

Nuclear waste – the radioactive waste left over as a by-product of nuclear power generation.

Nucleus – the core of an atom, made up of protons and neutrons (except hydrogen, which contains a single proton).

Observed brightness – the brightness of a star, dependent on its intrinsic brightness and distance from Earth.

Ozone layer – the layer of gas in the upper atmosphere that absorbs ultraviolet radiation.

Parallax – the apparent movement of an object; movement is actually caused by motion of the observer.

Peer review – the process by which new scientific ideas and discoveries are validated by other scientists.

Photon – a 'packet' of energy carried by electromagnetic radiation.

Photosynthesis – the chemical process that takes place in green plants where water combines with carbon dioxide to produce glucose using light energy.

Potential difference (voltage) – the difference in electrical charge between two charged points.

Pressure – force per unit area.

Proton – a positively charged particle found in the nucleus of an atom.

Radiation – energy carried by gamma radiation or by a stream of particles such as neutrons, alpha particles or beta particles.

Real image – an image produced by rays of light meeting at a point; an image that can be focused on a screen.

Glossary of Key Words

Red shift – the shift of light towards the red part of the visible spectrum; shows that the Universe is expanding.

Reflection – the change in direction of a wave as it hits a surface.

Refraction – the change in direction and speed of a wave as it passes from one medium to another.

Renewable – resources (e.g. energy sources) that will not run out or can be replaced.

Resistance – the measure of how hard it is to get a current through a component at a particular potential difference / voltage.

Resultant force – the total force acting on an object (the effect of all the forces combined).

Risk – the danger (normally to health) associated with a procedure, action or event.

Sidereal day – the time it takes the Earth to rotate 360°.

Solar day – a full 24 hours.

Static electricity – electricity that is produced by friction and doesn't move.

Supernova – an exploding star.

Tectonic plate – huge sections of the Earth's crust that move in relation to one another.

Transformer – an electrical device used to change the potential difference / voltage of alternating currents.

Transverse – a wave where the vibrations are at 90° to the direction of energy transfer.

Universe – a collection of galaxies.

Velocity – an object's speed and direction.

Velocity–time graph – a graph showing velocity against time taken; the gradient of the line represents acceleration.

Voltage (potential difference) – the difference in electrical charge between two charged points.

Wavelength – the distance between corresponding points on two adjacent disturbances (waves).

HT ALARA (As Low As Reasonably Achievable) – a policy of minimising risk while still providing benefits.

Angular magnification – a means of measuring the magnification based on the angle of rays of light from an object compared to the angle the image appears to make.

Chain reaction – a reaction, e.g. nuclear fission, that is self-sustaining.

Ecliptic – the apparent path the Sun traces out along the sky.

Hubble's Law – a law that states that the further away a galaxy is, the faster it is moving away from us.

Isotopes – atoms of the same element that contain different numbers of neutrons.

Magnetic field – the lines of force surrounding a magnet or the Earth.

Nuclear fission – the splitting of atomic nuclei, which is accompanied by a release in energy.

Nuclear reactor – the place where fission takes place in a nuclear power station.

Precautionary principle – experts and the public are consulted if scientific evidence is uncertain and the risks are unknown; the costs and benefits are then weighed up.

Subduction – when an oceanic plate is forced under a continental plate.

Uranium – a radioactive element often used as nuclear fuel.

Answers to Practice Questions

Module P1

1. A2, B3, C4, D1.
2. A, C, E.
3. a) Earth's crust is divided into **tectonic** plates.
   b) i)–iii) **In any order:** Plates slide past each other; Plates move away from each other; Plates move towards each other.
4. a) **Convection** currents in the **mantle** cause **magma** to rise and form new oceanic crust.
   b) Seafloor spreading.
5. 5000 million years old.
6. a) The Solar System began when **dust** and **gas** clouds were pulled together by **gravity** which created intense **heat**.
   b) **Nuclear** fusion began and the Sun was born.
   c) Smaller masses also formed, which **orbit** the Sun.
7. a)–b) **In any order:** Planets; Asteroids; Comets; Moons.
8. Light years.
9. a)–b) **In any order:** Relative brightness; Parallax.
10. a) The red giant's core contracts and it becomes a planetary **nebula**.
    b) The star's core cools and contracts further, becoming a **white** dwarf.
    c) It cools further to become a **black** dwarf.
11. If a source of light is moving away from us, the **wavelengths** of light are **longer** than if the source was stationary.
12. The Big Bang theory.

Module P2

1. a) A **beam** of electromagnetic radiation contains **packets** of energy called **photons**.
   b) Radiation energy travels from a source known as an **emitter** to a **detector**.
2. a) Intensity depends on the number of **photons** delivered per **second** and the amount of **energy** each **packet** contains.
   b) A
   c) i)–iii) **In any order:** Photons spread out; Photons are reflected; Photons are absorbed.
3. a)–b) **Any two from:** Ultraviolet rays; X-rays; Gamma rays.
4. a)–b) **Any two from:** Sunburn; Ageing of the skin; Mutations in the cell which can lead to cancer; Radiation poisoning.
5. a) The ozone layer.
   b) It absorbs ultraviolet radiation before it reaches Earth.
   c) Harmful amounts of radiation would get through and living organisms would suffer cell damage.
   d) Ultraviolet radiation causes **reversible** chemical changes in the upper atmosphere.
6. a) Carbon dioxide levels stayed constant because animals and plants recycled it.
   b) i)–ii) **In any order:** Burning fossil fuels; Deforestation.
7. a)–c) **In any order: Climate change:** Crops may not grow in some areas; **Extreme weather:** Hurricanes; Drought; **Rising sea levels:** Melting ice caps; Sea levels rising; Low-lying land flooding.
8. a) As Low As Reasonably Achievable.
   b) Measures should be taken to make the risks as small as possible, whilst still providing the benefits and taking into account social, economic and practical implications.

Module P3

1. a) i)–iii) **In any order:** Alpha; Beta; Gamma.
   b) Alpha.
   c) i)–ii) **Any two from:** Cancer treatment; Sterilising surgical instruments; Sterilising food.
2. a) False.
   b) True.
   c) False.
   d) False.
   e) True.
3. Electricity is generated from another energy source such as fossil fuels or nuclear power.
4. a) i)–ii) **Any two from:** Wind power; Hydroelectric power; Solar power.
   b) i)–ii) **Any two from:** Kinder to the environment; Cheaper; Will not run out like fossil fuels.
5. A1, B3, C5, D4, E2.
6. a) A chain reaction occurs when there's enough **fissile** material to prevent too many **neutrons** escaping without being absorbed.
   b) The amount of material needed for a chain reaction is called **critical** mass.
7. a) Fuel rods.
   b) It transfers heat energy from the reactor to the heat exchanger, where it heats water and turns it into steam.
   c) Control rods prevent the chain reaction getting out of control.

Answers to Practice Questions

Module P4

1. **a)–b) In any order:** Speed; Direction of travel.
2. $\frac{20m}{5s} = 4 m/s$
3. The speed of an object at a particular point in time.
4. **a)** A 3; B 2; C 1.
   b) $\frac{20m}{4s} = 5 m/s$
5. To make sure drivers don't exceed the speed limit and that they rest for suitable amounts of time.
6. The resistive force between two objects as they slide past one another.
7. add up; subtract; resultant force.
8. 1500kg x 45m/s = 67 500kg m/s
9. **a) i)–iii) Any three from:** Seat belts; Crumple zones; Motorcycle and bicycle helmets; Air bags.
   b) They increase the time of impact.
10. C
11. $\frac{1}{2}$ x 1200kg x (12m/s)^2 = $\frac{1}{2}$ x 1200 x 144 = 86 400J
12. It remains the same.
13. **a)** 18N x 8m = 144J
    b) 144J
    c) $144 = \frac{1}{2}$ x 2kg x V^2
       $144 = V^2$
       $V = \sqrt{144}$
           = 12m/s

Module P5

1. **a)** The two materials will repel each other.
   b) The two materials will attract each other.
2. ─┤├─
3. **a)** Direct; Alternating.
   b) i)–ii) In any order: It's easier to generate; It can be distributed more efficiently.
4. **a)** Voltage
   b) (Greater)
5. **a)** $\frac{15V}{5A} = 3\Omega$
   b) 0.6A x 20Ω = 12V
   c) More energy is transferred from the charge flowing through a greater resistance because it takes more energy to push the current through the resistor.
6. **a)–b) In any order:** Moving the magnet out of the coil; Moving the other pole of the magnet into the coil.
7. **a)** To change the voltage of an alternating current.
   b) When two coils of wire are close to each other, a changing magnetic field in one coil can induce a voltage in the other. Alternating current flowing through the primary coil creates an alternating magnetic field which induces an alternating current in the secondary coil.
   c) 20V
8. **a)** Joules
   b) Because a joule is a very small amount of energy.
   c) 40W x 30s = 1200J
   d) 1.8kW x 0.5h = 0.9kWh
9. **a)** $\frac{1600}{2000}$ x 100 = 80%
   b) $\frac{60}{200}$ x 100 = 30%
   c) $\frac{260}{400}$ x 100 = 65%

Module P6

1. **a)** Transverse
   b) Longitudinal.
2. A Amplitude; B Wavelength.
3. Frequency = $\frac{300\,000\,000 m/s}{200m}$ = 1 500 000Hz
4. **a)** A wave is refracted when it crosses a boundary between one medium and another. The wave's frequency stays the same, but there is a change in wavelength. This leads to a change in wave speed, which causes the wave to change direction.
   b) B and C
5. **a)** The light can't escape from the medium and is reflected.
   b) Total internal reflection.
6. Electromagnetic waves can travel through empty space but sound waves need a medium (solid, liquid or gas) to travel through.
7. 1 B; 2 A; 3 D; 4 C.
8. **a)** Digital signal
   b) Because digital signals only have two states, on (1) or off (0), so they can still be recognised despite any noise that's picked up. This means any interference can be removed.

Answers to Practice Questions

Module P7

1. A sidereal day is a 360° rotation of the Earth and a solar day is 24 hours.
2. False
3. 24 hours and 49 minutes.
4. a) They are brought to a central point.

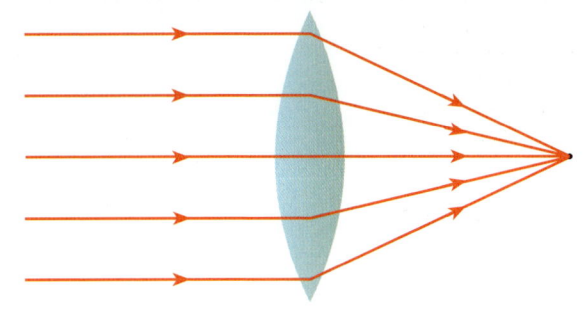

   b) 5 dioptres

5. a) apparent; parallax; close; larger; further
   b) 10 parsecs
6. It doesn't have a constant intrinsic brightness.
7. 40 megaparsecs.
8. C
9. Absolute zero.
10. a) 293
    b) 173
    c) 227
11. Convective zone – Where energy is transported to the surface by convection currents
    Core – The hottest part of the star
    Photosphere – Where energy is radiated into space.
12. a)–c) **In any order:** the particles passed straight through; the particles were deflected; the particles bounced back towards the source.

101

Notes

Notes

Index

A
Absolute temperature 86
ALARA 23
Aliens 12
Alpha particle scattering experiment 89
Amplitude 64
Analogue signals 70
Angular magnification 81
Atoms 28, 89
Attraction 52

B
Big Bang theory 12

C
Carbon cycle 21
Cepheid variable stars 84
Circuit symbols 53
Collisions 45
Continental drift 7
Current–potential difference graphs 55
Current 52, 53, 54
Curtis–Shapley debate 84

D
Diffraction 66, 90
Digital signals 70
Dinosaurs 13
Distance–time graphs 41–42

E
Earth 6–13, 76, 78
   Structure of 6
Electric generator 57
Electricity 32–33, 59
Electromagnetic induction 56
Electromagnetic spectrum 18, 68, 69
Elements 28
Energy 58
Erosion 6

F
Focal point 80
Forces 43, 44
Fossils 6
Frequency 64, 65, 68
Friction 43

G
Geohazards 7
Global warming 22
Gravitational potential energy 47
Greenhouse effect 20

H
Half-life 30
Hubble constant 85
Hubble, Edwin 84
Hubble's Law 12

I
Interference 67
Isotopes 28

K
Kinetic energy 46

L
LDRs 55
Lenses 80
Light speed 10
Lunar cycle 78
Lunar eclipse 79

M
Modulation 70
Momentum 44–45
Moon 78, 79

N
Nuclear fission 35
Nuclear reactors 35

O
Ozone layer 20

P
Parallax 10, 82
Parallel circuits 56
Parsecs 83
Peer-review process 7
Photons 18, 19, 68
Photosynthesis 20
Planets 77
Power 57
Pressure 86

R
Radiation 18, 19, 20, 28, 31
   Background 29
   Ionising 19, 28
Ray diagrams 80
Reflection 66
Refraction 66
Renewable energy 33–34
Repulsion 52
Resistance 43, 54

S
Safety devices 45
Sankey diagrams 33
Series circuits 55
Sidereal day 76
Solar day 76
Solar eclipse 79
Solar system 9
Speed 40–41
Stars 11, 77, 82, 83, 87, 88
   Spectrum 87
Static electricity 52
Sun 9, 20, 76, 79

T
Tectonic plates 7, 8
Telescopes 81, 90, 91
Thermistors 55
Transformers 58

U
Universe 10, 12

V
Velocity 40, 42
Velocity–time graphs 42

W
Wavelength 64, 65, 68
Waves 64–66
   Longitudinal 64
   Transverse 64